EL-HIBEH 1980

AMERICAN RESEARCH CENTER IN EGYPT REPORTS

Preliminary and Final Reports
of Archaeological Excavations in Egypt
from Prehistoric to Medieval Times

Volume 9

Published under the auspices of
THE AMERICAN RESEARCH CENTER IN EGYPT, INC.

ARCHAEOLOGICAL INVESTIGATIONS AT EL-HIBEH 1980: PRELIMINARY REPORT

by

Robert J. Wenke

with contributions by

M. Hassaan El-Hassaany, Tarek Naffie
Nanette Pyne, Richard Redding
Diana Ryesky, Wilma Wetterstrom

Undena Publications
Malibu 1984

Excavations, surface sampling, topographic mapping, and other archaeological and Egyptological researches were conducted at the site of el-Hibeh between February 11 and March 16, 1980. Results indicate that el-Hibeh, a large (approximately 13 hectares), walled "town" on the Nile's east bank across from el-Fashn, was first occupied in the late second millennium B.C. and remained an important site through much of the first millennium B.C. and into the first several centuries A.D. Excavations were conducted in stratified deposits in two areas of first millennium B.C. occupations, producing samples of ceramics, floral and faunal remains, architecture, and other artifacts. Aspects of the settlement's occupational history are reconstructed, and suggestions for future research are made.

To Maurice D. Schwartz, with appreciation.

Library of Congress Card Number 84-050291
ISBN 0-89003-154-1 (paper)
0-89003-155-x (cloth)
ISSN 0732-6432

Undena Publications, P. O. Box 97, Malibu, CA 90265 U.S.A.

TABLE OF CONTENTS

LIST OF TABLES

LIST OF MAPS

LIST OF FIGURES

LIST OF PLATES

PREFACE

The fieldwork phase of the el-Hibeh Archaeological Project began on February 10, 1980, with the transport from Cairo of our crew of nine and supplies about 140 km down the Nile's east bank (courtesy of Peter Drotleff and his fleet of Mercedes-Unimogs), to the village of el-Ograh, which lies approximately 1.2 kilometers north of the ancient settlement of el-Hibeh.

We took up residence in el-Ograh and commenced work at el-Hibeh on February 11th. Our modest crew size, small budget, and the terms of our research permit (which limited us to two shallow test excavations), restricted our season greatly, but we managed twenty-eight days of fieldwork, returning to Cairo on March 16th. At that time, most of the crew went back to the United States and my wife, Nanette M. Pyne, and I began six weeks' work in the Egyptian Museum, analyzing the el-Hibeh materials and sorting them preparatory to the artifact division.

Difficulties in exporting the textile, floral, faunal, glass, and other artifacts have delayed publication until this time. These artifacts finally arrived in Seattle in April 1982, and although their analysis is by no means complete, I have elected to publish a preliminary report so as to make public most of our findings. More detailed artifact analyses are currently underway and will be published when completed.

Another factor in the decision to publish this report in preliminary form is that circumstances have conspired to make an early resumption of the el-Hibeh project impossible. Thus, we cannot assume that we shall soon make additional excavations that will allow us to treat more fully the evidence and questions addressed in preliminary form here.

Archaeologists and Egyptologists typically have many people to thank for the success of their projects, and our list is particularly long. Dr. Shehata Adam, the former director of the Egyptian Antiquities Organization, helped us through some critical permit and security-clearance problems. Dr. Mohammed Saleh, director of the Egyptian Museum, graciously permitted us to export a sample of artifacts to the United States for technical analysis, and Dr. Mary Ellen Lane arranged the export. Mr. M. Mohsen, former director of the Egyptian Museum, arranged space and supervisory personnel for our work at the Museum.

In our dealings with the Egyptian Antiquities Organization, we were fortunate to have the help of Dr. Ali el-Khuli. In the field we were supervised and assisted with great cordiality and skill by Miss Nadia Ashur, by Mahmoud Hamsa, Chief Inspector for Middle Egypt, and by M. Mohsen of the Beni Suef office of the Antiquities Organization.

We are also grateful to the American Research Center in Egypt, and to Dr. Paul Walker, Dr. James Allen, Amira Khattab, Mai Trad, Attiya Habachi, and other A.R.C.E. staff members, all of whom provided project-saving help at one time or another.

I am grateful to the National Science Foundation for Grant BNS-79-24742, which supported part of our project, and, especially, to Mr. Maurice Schwartz, who, at the request of my co-director, Cynthia M. Sheikholeslami, donated most of the money to fund the field-season, and has also made possible the export of the artifacts and publication of this volume. We owe a great debt to him—as do many other Near Eastern archaeologists who have been the recipients of his generosity. The participants in the fieldwork, namely, Douglas Brewer, Jeffrey Cooper, John Leier, Janet Long, Marie Hanley, Russell Hanley, Nanette M. Pyne, and Cynthia Sheikholeslami, merit high marks. Despite a mudbrick house without heat, electricity, or water, and a cook with an unshakable faith in the nutritive powers of garlic, they did superbly. We are all especially grateful to Nanette M. Pyne, who travelled each weekend from Cairo, by taxi, boat, and donkey to bring us everything from cylinders of butagaz to chocolate.

All of us would also like to thank the people of el-Ograh, who met us with cordiality and kindness, worked for us with industry, and taught us much about Egypt.

Finally, our gratitude to Prof. Jere Bacharach, Department of History, University of Washington, and truly an *Amicus Curiae*, to whose administrative efforts this book owes its existence.

June 1982   Robert J. Wenke
                                                Department of Anthropology
                                                  University of Washington
                                                     Seattle, Washington

I. INTRODUCTION

The el-Hibeh archaeological project was designed to be a contribution both to the reconstruction of Egypt's culture history and to general analyses of the evolution of complex societies.

El-Hibeh's importance for these research objectives is tied to three factors: 1) its location (Map 1.1) in Middle Egypt at the "natural" juncture of Upper and Lower Egypt, so that it was at the point at which forces of political unity and fragmentation in Egypt repeatedly met; 2) its diverse periods of occupation, which spanned the political upheavals of the 21st Dynasty, the revival of Egypt's political fortunes under Shoshenq I, the Saite triumph, the Persian invasion, and the reshaping of Egypt under the Ptolemies; and 3) its size (Map 1.2) and highly varied settlement history—specifically, that it was at various times a large town, a fort, a "temple-town," and the home of a community of priests.

Our major research objectives were to make maps, surface collections, and excavations, and to conduct other researches at el-Hibeh so that we could reconstruct its settlement history and domestic economy and relate this information to Egyptian culture history. Ultimately, we sought to bring the whole to bear on the more fundamental issues of why ancient states and empires developed when, where, and in the forms that they did.

Obviously, one does not resolve major anthropological and historical questions such as these with a month's research by a small crew at a single site. Our work constitutes only an initial step towards our goals, and we can hardly speak with authority on the many important research problems raised in this report. But the formulation of testable hypotheses and the construction of explanations of Egypt's cultural history require, initially at least, the patient accumulation of precise forms of evidence, and we think we have made some progress in this regard.

A. Theoretical Context

It has long been a major premise of explanatory archaeology that our understanding of general cultural evolutionary processes can be advanced by analyzing the developmental similarities and differences exhibited by ancient civilizations (Steward 1949; Adams 1966; Flannery 1972; Harris 1979). And in this regard, one of the most important aspects of Egypt's archaeological record is the contrasts it offers to other early "civilizations." For example, although it paralleled Mesopotamia, China, and other areas in its broad evolutionary pattern, Egypt was *apparently* quite different in the rapidity with which it produced state-level political systems (Trigger 1979:42) and in its dispersed, largely non-urban settlement patterns (Butzer 1976:57-80; Bietak 1979; cf. Kemp 1977).

In the case of el-Hibeh, we were specifically interested in mapping and excavating this large settlement to produce evidence with which to investigate some of the major cultural

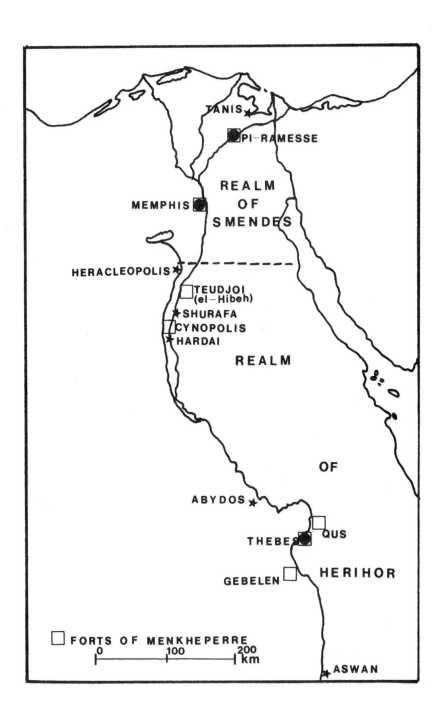

MAP 1.1
Egypt's Probable Political Divisions in the
Renaissance Era and 21st Dynasty (after Kitchen 1973).

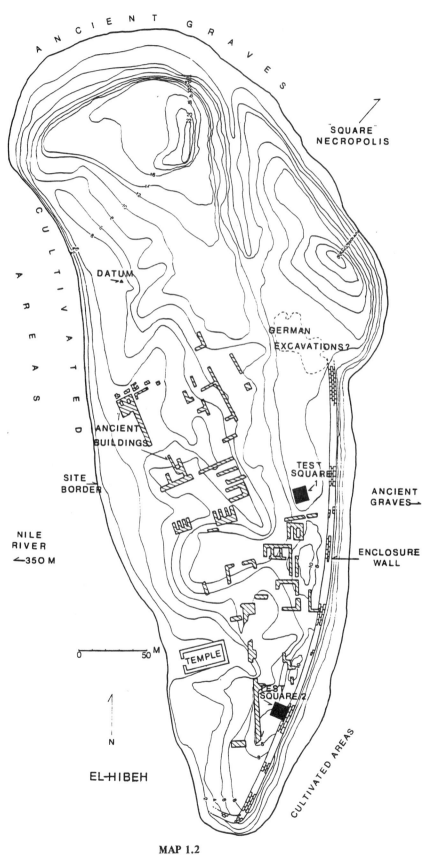

MAP 1.2
Topographic Map of el-Hibeh.

changes Egypt experienced during the first millennium B.C.—changes possibly involving factors that were potent agents of cultural transformation not only in Egypt but in other early civilizations as well.

It was in the first millennium B.C. and early first millennium A.D., for example, that population densities in the Nile Valley and Egypt as a whole increased rapidly, so that by the first few centuries A.D. densities in most areas may have been three or four times those of the Old Kingdom (Butzer 1976:84-85). The relationship between demographic and cultural change is probably not as direct as many scholars have suggested (e.g., Boserup 1965), but it is clear that, at some level, understanding the great transformations of history will require close analysis of demographic change (Smith and Young 1972; O'Connor 1972; Cowgill 1975). Yet, in Egypt few excavations and regional surveys have been conducted in such a way that we can estimate with precision the country's long and complex demographic history.

Some of the most interesting changes in first millennium B.C. Egypt involve variability in settlement patterns—which are comparatively accurate and accessible archaeological reflections of changing administrative and economic systems. The Nile Valley's rather homogenous agricultural environment, its "protection" from major outside influences by virtue of its desert borders, and the efficient communications and transportation channel provided by the river itself, all seem to have produced over many millennia settlement patterns characterized by few cities or towns, many essentially functionally redundant villages, and some specialized military, administrative, and religious settlements. Too few relevant excavations and surveys have been accomplished to be able to answer the most important questions about the origins and nature of Egyptian "urbanism" (reviewed in Helck 1975, Kemp 1977, and Bietak 1979), but recent analyses of the available evidence point to a vastly increased pace of urbanism, in the form of population aggregation and settlement differentiation, beginning in the last New Kingdom and extending to the first millennium A.D. (reviewed in Butzer 1976 and Bietak 1979). The highly variable appearance of "urbanism" in both Old and New World ancient cultures (reviewed in Wheatley 1971, Sjoberg 1960, and Hammond 1972) suggests that urbanization, at least in this sense of population aggregation and settlement functional differentiation, was only one of several ways of meeting a variety of economic, social, and political needs—needs that apparently were not strong in early Egypt or that were initially met in other ways. Precisely what factors produced rapid and pervasive urbanization in some ancient societies and not in others could be understood much more clearly if we had a more precise record of the nature and extent of Egyptian settlement patterns in periods when urbanization seems finally to be a major trend in Egypt.

El-Hibeh came to prominence during this era of increasing urbanization, and thus it is possible that many of the factors that operated generally to produce the first wave of Egyptian urbanization are reflected in the material remains at this site. These issues are discussed in more detail below as they relate to our work at el-Hibeh.

Another general problem involving el-Hibeh and its era concerns the nature of developmental cycles in ancient states and empires. When one addresses the problem of the *origins* of states and empires, one is led inexorably to the problem of the *functioning* of these early political systems. Numerous scholars have noted that typical of many preindustrial empires are developmental cycles in which periods of population growth, rising economic productivity, and increasing political integration alternate regularly with periods of demographic, technological, economic, and political decline and collapse (Steward 1949; Lattimore 1951; Eisenstadt 1967; Adams 1981; Wenke 1975-76).

In Egypt, these periods of collapse seem often to have involved the almost "natural" disintegration of the country into the traditional upper and lower halves, as the central government weakened. It is difficult to determine how many times this cycle of unification and fragmentation occurred, but there seem to have been several such oscillations.

Obvious parallels to this situation can be found in Mesopotamia, where city-states repeatedly banded together into imperial political systems, only to revert time and time again to warring component cities.

El-Hibeh is particularly significant when considered in the context of these kinds of imperial developmental cycles:

> From the 19th year of Ramesses XI (c. 1080 B.C.), all of Egypt and Nubia were divided into two great provinces, each under a chief whose common link and sole superior was the pharaoh. The boundary point was at El-Hibeh which became the northern base of the Theban ruler. Thus, under the last of the Ramesses a basic political pattern was established that was to last for over three centuries, through the 21st Dynasty and down to Prince Osorkon and the final collapse of the fractured unity of post-imperial Egypt (Kitchen 1973:251).

In summary, then, el-Hibeh can be viewed as a significant source of evidence about the great demographic and political shifts that are the warp and weft of cultural evolution in Egypt.

In our fieldwork during the 1980 season we concentrated on four activities: 1) construction of a topographic map of the site, in order to establish a context within which to interpret our surface collections and excavated materials, and in order to produce a permanent record of the site (which is still threatened by looting and *sebakh* removal); 2) collection of surface samples of artifacts in order to identify all periods of occupation and to reconstruct el-Hibeh's later occupational history; 3) excavation of stratified cultural deposits in a manner such that we could produce a seriated ceramics sequence for interpreting surface collections and el-Hibeh's relationship to other sites, and in order to gather information about the site's contents and its earliest periods of occupation; and 4) a description of the 22nd Dynasty temple at the site.

Before considering the specifics of the archaeological work, let us consider el-Hibeh's general ecological and historical context, to provide a framework within which to interpret the archaeological data.

B. Ecological Context

El-Hibeh's occupational history has, obviously, been in large part determined by its location and physical environment. The site was constructed on outcrops of the Middle Eocene limestone scarp that closely bounds the Nile between the latitudes of Beni Suef and Manfalut. This scarp runs at a widely varying distance from the Nile floodplain, with many spurs, indentations, and promontories, some rising to 250 meters above floodplain level to the east of el-Hibeh.

The floodplain immediately to the west of el-Hibeh, between the site and the Nile, varies between about 300 and 900 meters in width. Before the Nile was dammed, seasonal flooding around el-Hibeh was such that the 22nd Dynasty temple on the site's western edge was occasionally flooded. Villagers report that the temple has been flooded twice since it was last cleared in 1913/14 (Ranke 1926), and our excavations in 1980 revealed that the temple floor was covered by over a meter of unstratified silts and clays. Changes in the Nile floods have been so great since the High Dam was built that palm trees that previously flourished along el-Hibeh's western side are dying or are dead for lack of water. The area is now, and has been for at least the last several millennia, hyperarid, and all agriculture is dependent upon the Nile (Butzer 1976:39-40).

Plant and animal remains from el-Hibeh are discussed below, but some preliminary statements about the agricultural economy and ecology of the site's periods of occupation are appropriate here.

Although there may well have been a high degree of economic exchange between Middle Egyptian towns and cities during el-Hibeh's periods of occupation, the settlement was probably still dependent on its own agricultural resources for much of its food. And variability in productivity was in large part determined by fluctuations in Nile floods. Butzer (1976:30) interprets the evidence to show "a sustained decline of Nile flood levels after perhaps 1200 B.C. on a scale sufficient to promote floodplain dessication, with net aggradation not in evidence again until well into the Christian era." Within that period there may have been substantial annual variations, however. Tousson (1923), Brooks (1949), and Said (1981:92), for example, note evidence of high floods about 500 B.C.

For the citizens of el-Hibeh, marked changes in Nile flood levels probably would have had considerable impact. The cultivable strip between the site and the east bank of the Nile has always been quite narrow, and if there were relatively low-level floods in several consecutive years, severe difficulties might have ensued. However, by the 22nd Dynasty, el-Hibeh was probably sufficiently important that it could call on other settlements, including those on the west bank, for some of its food to even out such resource disparities through redistribution. The site includes many large structures that probably functioned as granaries (Paribeni 1935:388).

Butzer has suggested that, in addition to a well-conceived bureaucracy and colonial exploitation, a major factor in the great population growth in the Ptolemaic era may have been the invention of the *sāqiyyah* (animal-powered water wheel), which allowed intensive irrigation to compensate for fluctuations in Nile floods (1976:91-2).

In most periods, cropping strategies in the areas around el-Hibeh probably revolved around winter cultivation of barley, wheat, beans, chick peas, and flax, followed by a summer crop of onions, lentils, and fodder crops in areas where irrigation was possible. With the introduction of the *sāqiyyah* in Ptolemaic times, the area around el-Hibeh probably began to look much like rural Egypt does today, a "checkerboard pattern of interwoven, irrigated, derelict, . . . and waterlogged fields" (Butzer 1976:48). Date palms were probably in continuous cultivation, and in later periods peaches and other fruit trees were grown (see Chapter V).

As is discussed below, our analyses show that el-Hibeh's agricultural resources were supplemented in all periods by fish, and to a lesser extent by game birds and animals.

C. Historical Context

History has no record of the founding of el-Hibeh. Mud-bricks stamped with the names of the High Priest of Amun at Karnak, Menkheperre (1035-986 B.C.) and his wife, Estemkheb, have been found in great numbers in the upper courses of the enclosure wall at el-Hibeh, overlaying bricks stamped with the name of Pinudjem (1070-1032 B.C.). On this basis it has been assumed (Wainwright 1927; Caminos 1958) that much of the site dates from the 21st Dynasty. But, as Kitchen notes (1973:248, n.32), "The discovery of the Wenamun papyrus at el-Hibeh . . . suggests that some fort or centre had been established there by Piankh [C. 1094-1064 B.C.] or even Herihor [C. 1100-1094 B.C.] before the buildings of 21st-dynasty date." (Dates used here and below are from Kitchen [1973]).

As is discussed below, the archaeological evidence indicates that el-Hibeh was a substantial settlement well before the first years of the 21st Dynasty, but its earliest occupations have never been securely dated.

Kitchen notes (1973:248, n.32) that el-Hibeh was situated at a strategic point along the Nile and was able to control traffic passing southward. The resettlement and possible expansion of el-Hibeh by the rulers of the 21st Dynasty may well have been motivated by this consideration.

Sheikholeslami (Sheikholeslami and Wenke 1978) has recently summarized el-Hibeh's history. She notes that during the 21st and 22nd Dynasties, the northern political boundary of Upper Egypt was apparently near el-Hibeh (Wainwright 1927; Caminos 1958). The Harpenese correspondence (which refers to the town of P3 *ihy*, "the camp") deals with matters to the south of the town (mentioning the viceroy of Kush). El-Hibeh was selected as the site of a temple dedicated to Amun Great of Roarings (referring to river rapids?) by Seshonk I of the 22nd Dynasty, perhaps at the conclusion of his Palestinian campaign. His son, Iuput, the High Priest of Amun at Karnak, is also mentioned in the temple texts, and Osorkon I is named in an addition to the original structure (Kamal 1901; Daressy 1902; Ranke 1926). At this time the site seems to have been a stop on the route from Upper Egypt to the Levantine coast.

The lengthy inscription of Osorkon, the High Priest of Amun at Karnak, on the Bubastite Portal at the Temple of Karnak (ca. 850 B.C.) records that he resided in "The Crag" (T3 *dhnt*, one of el-Hibeh's ancient names) and journeyed from there southward to Thebes to officiate in ceremonies at the Temple of Karnak (Caminos 1958; Sheikholeslami and Wenke 1978).

During the eighth century B.C., Upper Egypt was divided into three spheres of influence, dominated by Thebes, Hermopolis, and Heracleopolis, and el-Hibeh may have been at the border of the territories of Hermopolis and Heracleopolis. And since the Thebans at times may have been allies of the Heracleopolitans, with the citizens of Hermopolis being an opponent of both, el-Hibeh would have been in a crucial political location (Sheikholeslami and Wenke 1978).

Until the Nubian conqueror Piye (Piankhy) invaded el-Hibeh in 734 B.C. (Baer 1973), the town was dominated by the important Delta chieftain Tefnakht, who controlled most of Lower Egypt. After el-Hibeh surrendered to Piye, the site may have been much reduced in population or even abandoned for about fifty years.

After this period of decline, el-Hibeh again became an administrative post under the

Saites. Affairs of one of the town's priestly families are documented from the Saite through the early Persian periods (ca. 664-515 B.C.) in Papyrus Rylands IX (The Petition of Peteese, Griffith 1909). In the first half of the 26th Dynasty (ca. 664-595 B.C.), Upper Egypt was apparently controlled by officials in Heracleopolis, for whom el-Hibeh, then known as Teudjoi (*T3y.w d3y* "their [i.e., Menkheperre and Estemkheb] walls"), may have been an inspection post. Although settlers were coming to el-Hibeh from Thebes, the temple at el-Hibeh had fallen into disrepair. The temple was restored at the beginning of the 26th Dynasty by one member of this priestly family, who received income by virtue of his position in its clergy (Griffith 1909). During much of this period the town seems to have been in decline, with the priests eking out a living by cultivating fields on an island in front of the temple. With Peteese's appeal to the Persian satrap (ca. 520 B.C.), our major textual evidence for the history of the site comes to an end (Sheikholeslami and Wenke 1978).

El-Hibeh is identified with the Greek town of Ancyropolis. Although previous excavations at el-Hibeh have concentrated on the later levels (primarily on the Ptolemaic levels but on the Roman and presumed Coptic periods as well), they have not been systematic enough to construct the site's later development. In the Ptolemaic period, some sort of town planning may have been introduced, since a more regular layout of buildings seems evident (Paribeni 1935). And although some of the houses and granaries of this period have been excavated, the results of these excavations are incompletely published (Ranke 1926; Paribeni 1935). In the Ptolemaic and Roman period, the necropolis—compromising several distinct areas to the east of the site—seems to have served many west bank communities (Sheikholeslami and Wenke 1978).

The bulk of the Greek papyri from el-Hibeh (recovered from cartonnage enclosing mummies buried in the adjacent necropolis) dates from the middle of the reign of Ptolemy II Philadelphus to the end of the reign of Ptolemy III Eurgetes (ca. 265-221 B.C.). Several date from the 1st to the 3rd centuries A.D., including a tax-list of the villages in the Heracleopolite nome in the 1st and 2nd centuries A.D. The latest papyrus, dated A.D. 335, is a levy on Ancyropolis for hay to support a bakery in Babylon (Old Cairo). Among the documents whose provenance can be established, those originating from Oxyrhynchus heavily outnumber the few from the Arsinoite nome or the Heracleopolite nome itself. Of those originating from the Heracleopolite nome, some were written in the Koite toparchy of that nome, which included el-Hibeh, and show el-Hibeh as linked to an administrative center at nearby Phebichis. The documents include a postal register for a bureau that may have been located at Phebichis and the record of a man from Ancyropolis (el-Hibeh) paying a crown tax in wheat at Phebichis. In A.D. 176-80, nine column bases with drums and capitals were delivered to a palaestra at Heracleopolis from quarries at el-Hibeh, and there are also references to linen weavers at Ancyropolis in A.D. 309-310 (spindles were found at the site by the German expedition) (Sheikholeslami and Wenke 1978).

Although these papyri from cartonnage make only scanty reference to el-Hibeh during the Graeco-Roman periods, they do indicate continued habitation of the town and something of its relationship to other communities in the region. The demotic papyri recovered from the cartonnage found at el-Hibeh have not been published.

Together, these various Pharaonic and Ptolemaic historical sources raise the possibility that relatively low population densities in Middle Egypt during the early first millennium B.C. made this area a target for colonization and imperial development. Theban settlers are documented at el-Hibeh during the 25th Dynasty, and the Ptolemies are known to have settled large numbers of military personnel in this region.

II. ARCHAEOLOGICAL INVESTIGATIONS

A. The Topographic Map

The preliminary topographic map (Map 1.2) is based on 227 mapped points—fewer than would be required for adequate representation of the site's convolutions. Only 227 points were located because it was decided early in the project that our very limited resources would best be concentrated mainly on the excavations. El-Hibeh has been so badly looted that a precise topographic record of its interior areas would be for the most part not a record of the architecturally produced surficial discomformities but of the pits, holes, and mounds left by thousands of years of looting and wholesale transport of material from the site to agricultural fields. In short, during the 1980 season we tried to produce a preliminary map that could be used to locate precisely our excavations and surface collections and that would serve as a basis for mapping in future seasons.

The permanent datum point for the map is a cross, chiseled in and painted in black enamel on limestone bedrock protruding from the northwest side of el-Hibeh (Map 1.2).

B. Site Surface Sampling

It was originally intended that many samples of surface debris would be collected on the basis of a random transect sampling design that has been demonstrated elsewhere (Plog 1976, 1978; Mueller, ed. 1975) to be one of the most efficient for sampling complex environments. But it soon became evident that looting and site disturbances were such that our main objective in taking the samples could not be met; rather than representing a record of the site's occupational history, surface samples reflected primarily the depths to which looters had gone to rob tombs and the strata that *sebakhiin* had revealed in removing sediments for use on adjoining fields. Worse, it became apparent during excavations (see below) that a common construction technique at el-Hibeh involved the wholesale transport of occupational debris from one part of the site to another to serve as foundations and building material for subsequent constructions. There are, for example, many large complexes of standing architecture whose walls were largely made up of pottery and debris from earlier occupations. Most buildings have been disturbed greatly by looters tunnelling through their floors. Thus it was not possible to date these structures easily, rendering some forms of analysis impractical. We had hoped, for example, to measure house sizes in order to produce data comparable to Kemp's (1977) summary statistics on house size at Amarna. But in the case of el-Hibeh, the long occupational history and lack of good chronological controls on the architecture (in contrast to the situation at Amarna) prevented meaningful statistical analyses of house size.

All Egyptian town sites—and most large archaeological sites everywhere—have suffered some degree of disturbance, of course, but el-Hibeh has suffered more than most.

Over fifty surface samples *were* collected, however, most of them comprising sherds and other artifacts taken from beneath building complexes in levels exposed by looters, or from the surfaces of apparently undisturbed areas or other locations we thought potentially informative.

Perhaps the most significant of these samples were those taken from levels underlying the enclosure wall. Neither of the test excavations (which were both located inside the enclosure wall) reached the site's basal level, but *sebakhiin* activities have exposed the foundation of the enclosure wall at many points along its southeast portion. There, directly beneath courses of bricks stamped with names of rulers of the 21st Dynasty, are strata of occupational debris exposed to a depth of at least 2.0 meters. It is not clear whether or not this represented the site's basal occupation.

Our permit did not allow excavations in this area, but it was possible to make several collections of ceramics from exposed strata. One of the surprising things about these ceramics was that they were almost exclusively one form and ware (Appendix 1, Type 117): a shallow, orange-to-buff colored plate, sand tempered and of only two lip designs. Virtually the only other ceramics recovered from beneath the wall were body sherds from coarse, chaff-tempered vessels, of which no rims or bases were found—despite many hours of searching. At no place was architecture visible in the sections exposed beneath the enclosure wall, which may mean that the 21st Dynasty settlement associated with the enclosure wall was constructed on the remains of an earlier settlement that had been thoroughly disturbed—possibly as a result of the 21st Dynasty constructions. Wall collapse and looters' debris have covered the enclosure wall's northern portion, so it is not possible to determine either the period or size of this earliest occupation of el-Hibeh.

The ceramics recovered from beneath the wall are, unfortunately, of a type thought to be quite long-lived. They appeared in the very lowest levels of our test excavations elsewhere on the site, but in disturbed context. There seem to be strong resemblances between el-Hibeh's orange-buff shallow bowls and those attributed to the 18th Dynasty at el-Amarna (Kelley 1976: Plate 67.3) and to the 18th through 19th Dynasties at Gurob (Kelley 1976: Plate 68.10). Essentially identical sherds were encountered during the 1980 season at Mendes (personal observation). At present, all that can be accurately said of this form is that most associations seem to be with late New Kingdom occupations; but, as noted, the type may well persist well into the Late Period.

We searched many exposed, disturbed areas of el-Hibeh for primary deposits bearing these orange-buff shallow bowls, with indeterminate results. Most of the standing architecture directly in back of the temple (Map. 1.2) was built on layers of refuse containing this pottery type—in fact, almost whole bowls were recovered from many buildings on the southern half of the site. But these building foundations seem to have been mainly transported and compacted secondary deposits, and nowhere did we find unambiguous primary deposits involving this particular pottery style.

In any case, the possibly late New Kingdom style of the pottery found under the enclosure wall and the substantial occupational strata in evidence beneath the wall raise the possibility that el-Hibeh was a considerable community in late Ramessid times; and that, rather than founding a new settlement, the 21st Dynasty rulers were circumvallating and expanding an existing one.

The few samples we retrieved from these pre-21st Dynasty occupations do not lend themselves to strong inferences, but the fact that most of the identifiable pottery we recovered from these levels was of just one form and ware may indicate that el-Hibeh may have been a "special-function" site, such as a military or administrative outpost.

As for the scores of other surface samples collected, their disturbed provenience suggests that they can provide little systematic evidence about el-Hibeh's occupational history. Certainly, they are not suitable for the purpose for which they were collected: to form the basis of a computerized interpolation map (SYMAP, Dougenik and Sheehan 1975) for reconstructing ceramic variability over the whole of el-Hibeh's surface.

Nonetheless, in the process of collecting and analyzing the surface samples, it was possible to formulate several somewhat general observations about el-Hibeh, none of which could be rigorously tested and confirmed, but which may be of interest to subsequent researchers at el-Hibeh.

First, it is clear that in many different periods people dug through occupational debris and into el-Hibeh's limestone foundation for the purpose of burying their dead. I counted over twenty-five shafts cut into the limestone bedrock, some more than 5 meters in depth, as measured from the site surface. Broken pieces of limestone sarcophagi litter some (especially the west central) areas of the site, as well as el-Hibeh's eastern desert periphery. I could detect no obvious spatial patterning of these grave shafts on the site itself. It is entirely possible that looters have missed some graves.

Second, there was no evidence of "public" buildings at el-Hibeh other than the 22nd Dynasty temple. We looked in all disturbed areas for protruding limestone blocks, exceptionally large walls, and concentrations of stamped bricks, but all visible building remains seem to be of a kind best described as "domestic," except for: a) what appear to be granaries of capacities that one might estimate as beyond the annual needs of even a large extended family; b) some rather extensive mud-brick constructions revealed in Test Square 1 (see below); and c) some undecorated but carefully worked limestone blocks forming the corner of a building partially visible in a looter's pit about 10 meters south of Test Square 1. Obviously the later occupations could be obscuring non-domestic, public architecture in the lower levels of el-Hibeh.

A third general observation concerns processes of site formation. Despite detailed studies of the cultural and non-cultural processes by which archaeological sites are formed (e.g., Schiffer 1976), comparatively little is known about these factors as they pertain to the settlements of later Egyptian antiquity (but see Bietak 1979). Based on my experiences in Mesopotamia, and on observations at other Egyptian sites, I suspect el-Hibeh is an example of modified "spiral stratigraphy": over the centuries the focus of occupation changed from area to area within the site, so that rather than a layer-cake like composition, contemporary buildings were distributed unevenly, at different elevations. Further stratigraphic complexities were probably introduced at el-Hibeh by the common Middle Eastern practice of using abandoned buildings as garbage bins.

Finally, it seems quite clear that at least some of the Roman period occupation of el-Hibeh was concentrated on the northern half of the site, for the distinctive high-fired red and black wares of these periods are found almost exclusively north of Test Square 1 (see below). The extremely disturbed nature of the site makes it unlikely that such wares are in fact present in substantial quantities on the southern half of the site and simply obscured by later deposits. In addition to these ceramic evidences, Paribeni's report (1935) suggests a rough north-south division in terms of epigraphic materials—although his directions and assessments are not made with any great precision:

> Quelli {papyrus fragments} rinvenuti nella parte Nord dello scavo sono per lo piu di scrittura greca corsiva de eta romana, mentre quelli raccolti dalle case della zona Sud intorno al tempio sono tutti demotici. (1935:398)

How much of this separation is an accident of the use of different secondary deposits, however, is impossible to say.

C. The Excavations

It was considered essential to our research objectives that excavations be conducted to produce stratified samples of pottery from which to create a pottery typology and seriation—and thus to relate el-Hibeh to other sites—and also to recover architecture, plant and animal remains, and other artifacts with which to reconstruct the site's occupational history.

These objectives could be met only in preliminary form because of the massive size of el-Hibeh relative to the limited resources of the 1980 season, and also because we were restricted by the terms of our permit to two test excavations.

Because of this latter consideration, we located the two test excavations in areas that were relatively undisturbed, yet were sufficiently close to disturbed areas that we could, by examining these disturbed areas, assure ourselves that the excavation unit would not encounter at a shallow depth the limestone outcrop on which the site is built. We also tried to locate areas for excavation that represented distinct but overlapping periods of occupation and that would provide some opportunity of reaching the site's earliest occupations. Another goal was to excavate in areas that represented contrasting activities (e.g., domestic residences vis-à-vis public architecture, etc.)

As noted, the site's northern two-thirds are littered with fragments of the distinctive high-fired wares of the Roman Period (see Appendix I, Types 100-105), but these ceramic and glass types do not appear in significant densities on the southern third. For that reason we located the first test excavation just south of the boundary between the Roman and presumably pre-Roman surface deposits, in the hope that occupations older than the Roman period would be encountered. Looters' pits on all sides of Test Square 1 (hereafter, "TS1") suggested that this area had at least 2 meters of occupational debris and that there was substantial mud-brick architecture at 1.2 meters beneath the surface.

The second test excavation (hereafter, "TS2") was located to the south of TS1 (Map 1.2) immediately adjacent to the enclosure wall, in the top courses of which are hundreds of bricks stamped with names of notables of the 21st Dynasty. It was hoped that this area would yield deposits contemporary with, and perhaps earlier than, the wall. Also, since TS1 was set in an area whose surface was marked with ash, bone, and apparent "domestic" ceramics—an area perhaps indicative of, in other words, domestic residences—we located TS2 near the enclosure wall so that we might perhaps encounter public architecture associated with the wall.

The orientation of TS1 was determined by the orientation of mud-brick walls visible at about 1.2 meters depth in adjacent looters' pits: the excavation was aligned so that if TS1 contained a building oriented with and of about the same size as the one in the looters' pit, this building's walls would cross the excavation square parallel to its baulks. TS2 was aligned with architectural features eroding from its surface and with the enclosure wall forming the east edge of the square.

Each excavation was begun as a 5 x 5 m square and subsequently expanded to the 10 x 10 m maximum size specified in our concession. An excavation unit of 10 x 10 m is often too large for precise stratigraphic control, but in both our test squares the preservation of architecture, floors, and other stratigraphic features was such that few problems were encountered in distinguishing and keeping separate the stratigraphic levels.

Before describing the excavation results, it may be useful here to note several points about our excavation tactics.

First, although the most useful general method of provenience control is to impose (either graphically or by staking) a grid on a site to provide the basis for a Cartesian coordinate system, this was not appropriate in the case of preliminary work at el-Hibeh. The fact that we were limited to two test excavations precluded any sense of a sampling design, and it was more important to orient our text excavations with regard to existing architecture and site disturbances than with the dictates of a grid. The test excavations were, of course, precisely located on the site map and can be referenced to a site grid if there are future seasons of fieldwork.

Second, because of the horizontal distance between our two test excavations, the complexity of the intervening stratigraphy, and for other reasons discussed below, it was not possible to make undoubted stratigraphic correlations between the two test excavations. The *probable* correlation of strata in the two test squares, however, has been suggested below.

The third informative point about our excavation strategy and tactics involves nomenclature. In the absence of standardized terms in Egyptian archaeology, we used in the traditional fashion the provenience designations of Level, Layer, Feature, Floor, etc. For recording convenience, features were given unique numbers as encountered, rather than tied to level numbers, as is sometimes done. The use of the concept "Lot," which is essentially equivalent to the concept of "Locus" (Joukowsky 1980:171), involves a certain arbitrariness. Lots are usually employed as the minimal provenience collective unit (Sharer and Ashmore 1979:246), such as different areas within the floor of a single building. Unless a clear reason exists for distinguishing lots, however, it is perhaps better to treat them as features. We occasionally collected such things as house floors in two different lots, even though no obvious differences between them could be discerned, on the grounds that such lots might show interesting variations in artifact, sediment, and faunal contents within a particular house or structure. But it should be noted that for purposes of statistical comparisons between, for example, the plant macrofossil contents of the different building levels described below, many of the individual lots should be combined.

Lots were numbered when first defined and retained that number through several excavation levels. They were drawn at each level so that volume estimates could be made.

Excavations proceeded insofar as was possible by cultural stratigraphy. Almost all deposits from floors, pits, and other features were screened through a 4 x 4 mm mesh, which recovered even such tiny objectives as beads and rodents' teeth. Samples of disturbed and redeposited layers were also screened. The workmen doing the screening were rotated occasionally to minimize biases in any one square. Sediment samples were collected from every feature and level, including those few that appeared sterile of any plant and animal remains. The sediments have still not been exported for final analysis, and we hope to dry-sort, float, and in other ways study them in Cairo in the future.

Test Square 1

Prior to excavation, diagnostic sherds (i.e., rims, bases, handles, decorated pieces, etc.) were collected from each quadrant of TS1. Removal of the top 10 cm of the weathered surface deposit revealed that the entire surface of the northeast quadrant of TS1 (hereafter TS1a) was redeposited cultural deposits. Subsequent excavations in 10 cm levels showed that TS1a comprised many layers of reeds separated by an equal number of layers of pottery-filled occupational debris. These layers were made up of a single or double thickness of reeds, separated from the next reed-layer by about 4 to 8 cm of occupational debris. The reeds were apparently not woven or bound; they seem to be rush-like plants, about 2 to 3 m long, and 5 mm in diameter, laid out in sheets.

Because this kind of layered construction was used all over el-Hibeh, from the earliest to the last occupations, it is necessary to speculate briefly on its significance. I can find no other reports of this precise construction technique in Egypt, although rebuilding on disturbed primary and secondary deposits is a fundamental form of Egyptian architecture. The most common foundation materials at Egyptian sites are layers of mud-brick, cut stone, piled mud, or a combination of these. Mud-brick, however, and piled mud both require vast amounts of water, and at el-Hibeh transporting either the water or bricks from factories near the water would have been laborious. It seems possible that the alternating layers of reeds and debris often used at el-Hibeh were cheap substitutes for these more substantial foundation materials. By "bonding" the reed-debris layers through orienting the reeds in different directions in successive layers—as is done with bricks—stable foundations could be constructed without manufacturing bricks. And the raw materials for the reed-debris foundations were virtually inexhaustible.

Experienced excavators of Near Eastern sites might wonder whether or not these reed-debris deposits are simply superimposed floors and roofs or refuse heaps, but this is not possible. The standardized thicknesses of these layers, their regular alternation, their homogenous contents, their lack of association with walls or floors, and their large area are just some of the attributes that distinguish them from superimposed occupational layers. Nonetheless, for the most part, artifact and sediment samples taken from these distinct construction layers were segregated, bagged, and labelled to preserve their different proveniences.

Excavations in TS1a continued through the reed-debris layers for about 30 cm, and examination of the profile for this unit (Figure 2.1) suggests that the area was being levelled off, either as the foundation for a structure or as covering for subterranean features. The former is questionable, as preservation at el-Hibeh is such that a structure of any permanence would likely be in evidence. But it is possible that the planned buildings never got beyond the foundation stage.

The idea that these reed-debris layers were laid down as a covering over subterranean

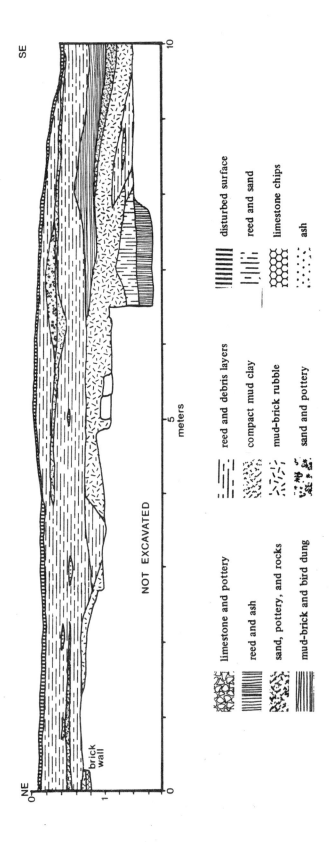

FIGURE 2.1

Profile of TS1a-TS1b, East Baulk

features—perhaps tombs—is intriguing. The undulating limestone on which el-Hibeh is built is honeycombed with tomb shafts, representing a variety of periods and methods of construction. Many of these have been looted, as is demonstrated by the large quantities of mummy bandages, sarcophagus fragments, and coffin boards that litter the site's surface, but some tombs probably remain undiscovered and intact.

When we encountered these thick layers of reed-debris construction on the surface of TS1, with no evidence of superimposed architecture, we considered the possibility that we would find intact tombs. But the several intervening periods of architecture required careful excavation and mapping, and we did not reach the underlying limestone layers in most areas of the unit. Although the several large pits in TS1 (see below) may be traces of burial shaft construction, we were not able to pursue this possibility because of the complex building levels in the lower depths of TS1.

Thus, the existence of intact tombs under the architecture of TS1 remains a possibility; it would seem to require something like this to account for the effort and costs invested in covering over these buildings.

The architectural succession at TS1 is complex and cannot be entirely understood without additional, extensive excavations. For this reason, we concentrated more on obtaining stratified sealed deposits of pottery, bones, etc., than on exposing architectural arrangements.

LEVEL 1 of TS1a was removed as a layer averaging about 8 cm thickness, somewhat thicker on the western half in order to level the excavation surface. There were a few areas of differential hardness, especially on the western half of the square, but the composition of the excavated material was the unvarying reed-debris sandwiched layers described above. No feature or lot assignments were made.

LEVEL 2 also averaged about 8 cm thickness, again somewhat thicker on the western half. There was no evidence of architecture, features, or primary cultural strata, the entire contents again consisting of several layers of reeds and debris. Samples were taken of ceramics, other artifacts, and sediments. A concentration of broken bricks appeared in a semicircle between .40 m and 1.5 m along the east baulk (measured from the northeast corner) covering an area of about 1.2 m². No lot or feature assignments were made.

LEVEL 3 was about 15 cm thickness, most of which was redeposited fill and the by now familiar layers of reeds and debris. But toward the bottom of this level, several concentrations of mud-brick fragments in linear patterns were found, and it appeared that we would encounter intact architecture at about 32-37 cm depth (all depth measurements in TS1 were made from the surface of the northwest corner of the square). No feature or lot assignments were made.

LEVEL 4, the top of which was approximately 40 cm below the site surface in each corner of the square, included the deposits associated with the upper courses of this architecture. Removal of these deposits revealed the complex illustrated in Figure 2.2. The fill in Lot 1 was predominantly the reed-debris layers, rather than intact primary deposits. Nonetheless, soil and artifact samples were taken and part of the lot was screened. Some large concentrations of what appeared to be pigeon dung were found toward the bottom of Lot 1.

Features 1 and 2 were defined in Level 4 (Figure 2.2), with Feature 1 eventually determined to be bricks in the top courses of Wall C, and Feature 2 comprising a dish-shaped

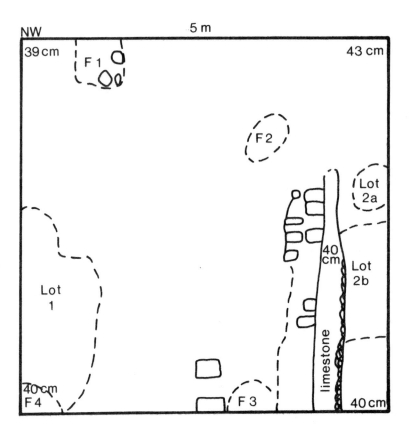

FIGURE 2.2
TS1a, Level 4.

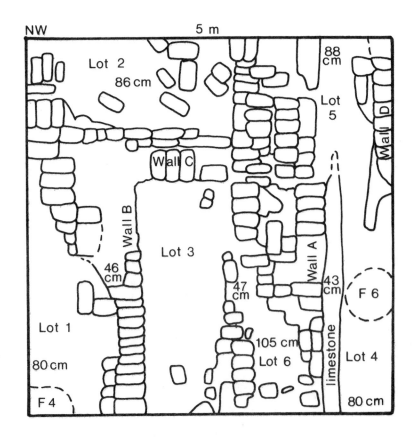

FIGURE 2.3
TS1a, Level 6, Building I.

pocket of ash, charcoal, and other sediments. Subsequently, Feature 3 was defined as another dish-shaped ash and charcoal concentration. Later excavations revealed that neither Features 1 nor 2 were primary deposits; both probably resulted from dumping baskets of fill taken from other areas of the site. Sediment samples were taken from these and all other features.

The depths-from-surface of various lots and features in Level 4 are indicated in Figure 2.2.

LEVEL 5 began as another removal of about 15 cm of reed-debris layers and other fill in TS1a, with the previously defined features being left in place. Feature 5 was defined as dish-shaped deposit with a maximum depth of about 9 cm, of fairly clean sand. At the bottom of Level 5 we reached an average depth of about 50 cm in TS1a, and the outlines of several courses of intact brickwork could be seen.

LEVEL 6 was then begun, revealing further the constructions of Building I (Figure 2.3). Lots 1, 2a, 2b, and 3 were taken down 5 cm, and Lot 2a bottomed out at about 51 cm, while the other lots continued. Lots 3 and 2b proved to have heavy concentrations of pottery, textiles, ash, and vegetable materials, and these appeared to be primary deposits. Lot 2a remained mainly reed-debris layers of secondary deposits. By excavating Lots 2a and 2b, the limestone "shelf" in TS1a (Figure 2.3) was shown to be bedrock, rather than quarried pieces put here in the course of construction.

With the top of LEVEL 7 we proceeded to remove deposits in lots associated with the different wall groups, since at that time we did not know whether we were inside or outside of one, two, or possibly more buildings.

Excavations revealed that Lots 5 and 6 bottomed out on mud-brick walls at depths of 88 cm and 105 cm respectively.

The bricks in the walls of Building I in TS1a and TS1d were quite uniform in size, as the following measurements for a sample of ten indicate:

39 x 18 x 11 cm	39 x 18 x 12 cm
39 x 18 x 11 cm	39 x 18 x 12 cm
38 x 18 x 11 cm	37 x 18 x 11 cm
37 x 17 x 11 cm	39 x 19 x 12 cm
39 x 18 x 12 cm	39 x 19 x 12 cm

Bricks in other areas of this structure showed some minor variability (the largest recovered was 41 x 18 x 12 cm), but the uniformity here was such that it is apparent that the bricks were all mould-made.

One of the bricks in Wall B of Building I was stamped with a cartouche, some elements of which could be identified (Appendix 3, Plate 2a). Since it was the only stamped brick recovered here, it was probably looted from the enclosure wall and used here long after that wall's construction.

LEVEL 8 excavations were concentrated on Lots 1, 2, 3, and 6, all of which continued to be jumbled layers with bones, pottery, textiles, and other refuse. Feature 6 was defined in this level as a very heavy concentration of reeds, bits of rope, pottery, and bones, that extended from about 85 to 91 cm depth in a circular area about 80 cm in diameter (Figure 2.3).

LEVEL 9 began with excavations in most of the previously defined lots, but concentrated in Lot 7, which was removed as a layer (from depth of 80 to 124 cm) in the area illustrated in Figure 2.4. This lot contained several papyri fragments (Appendix 3, Plate 1), a fragment of a faience "ring" (Appendix 4, Plate 1A), and some textiles.

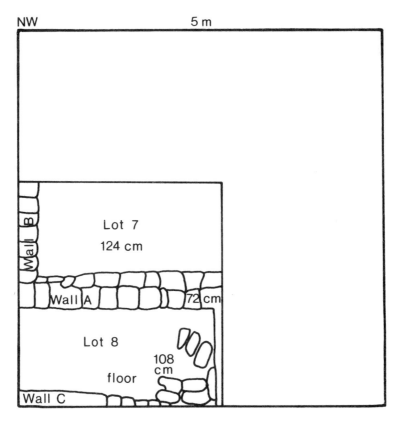

FIGURE 2.4
TS1a, Level 12, Building II.

LEVEL 10 excavations were concentrated on Lots 7 and 8, which contained the usual jumble of sherds, textiles, bones, and plant remains, all intermixed in a sandy sediment containing much ash and clay. Lot 8 contained a single bead and the bottom third of a faience figurine, as well as other debris. The bottom of Lot 8 was a hard plastered surface, probably a floor. It was reached by removal of the bricks in Wall B of Building I, and this floor seems to be associated with Building II, Wall A (Figure 2.4), which is an earlier construction than Building I. Additional inscribed papyri fragments (Appendix 3, Plate 1) were found in Lot 8 at a depth of about 93 cm.

LEVELS 11, 12, and 13 were excavations concentrated in the southwest corner of TS1a, in Lots 7 and 8, in order to clear and then penetrate the compact-mud "floor" encountered in Level 10. We were particularly interested in recovering samples of ceramics below this floor in order to extend our relative seriation of ceramic styles. Unfortunately, the area

FIGURE 2.5
TS1d, Level 3, Building I

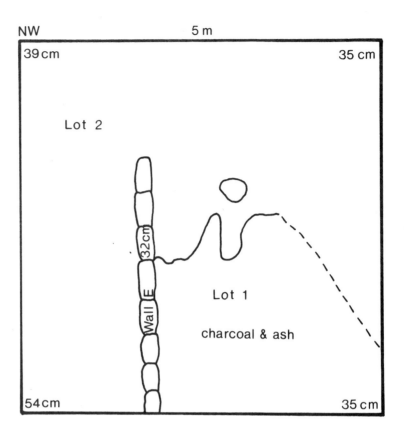

FIGURE 2.6
TS1d, Level 4, Building I

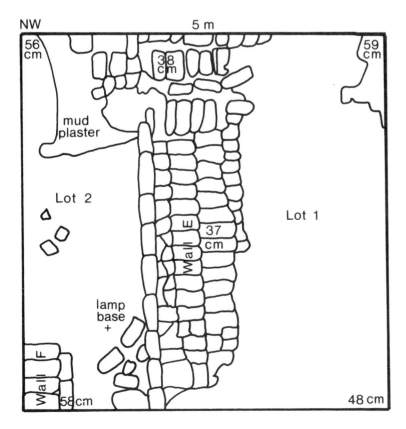

excavated proved to be mainly relatively "clean" fill, so that the samples of ceramics recovered were not large.

At this stage in our excavations, we had reached limestone bedrock at several places in TS1a, and it was clear that to interpret the architecture revealed so far, and to produce additional superimposed occupational levels, we would have to excavate other areas of TS1. Our resources simply were not adequate to excavate with good stratigraphic control the whole 10 x 10 meter area of TS1 simultaneously, so we decided to concentrate our efforts on TS1d and TS1b.

Excavations in LEVEL 1 of TS1d began with removal of the reed-debris layers encountered in TS1a, although in this case we removed them in just two layers based on the stratigraphic profile exposed in TS1a.

Near the bottom of LEVEL 2, at about 32 cm depth, we encountered the first courses of Wall E of Building I (Figure 2.5), other walls of which had been revealed in TS1a. Charcoal, ash, and reddened sediments in Lot 1 of TS1d suggest that parts of this building had been burned in place. The top of this lot contained reed fragments, sherds, and bones, but not as many textile fragments as in TS1a.

Excavation of LEVEL 3 at TS1d was concentrated on Lots 1 and 2, both of which contained unstratified deposits of bone, sherds, brick fragments, wood fragments, ash, shell, and other materials.

LEVEL 4 was also excavated mainly in Lots 1 and 2, the contents of these lots being much like they were at LEVEL 3. One notable find was the inscribed base of an oil lamp (Appendix 3, Plate 1), located at about 50 cm depth in Lot 2 (Figure 2.6). The disturbed context of this find, however, renders it only marginally useful as a chronological indicator.

Despite the excellent preservation of the brickwork in Building I, only a fragment of the floor associated with this building was visible in our excavations. It became clear from the shape of this floor and, more important, from the overall architectural layout, that Building I was no simple rectangular domestic residence.

Figure 2.7, in which TS1a and TS1d architecture is depicted as a unit (with that of TS1b, whose excavation is described below), shows that Building I is in fact a sizeable construction whose extent cannot be determined from our excavations. The thickness of the walls (up to 1.75 m), the narrow passageways between the walls, and the overall shape of the building do not much resemble the simple mud-brick houses still standing in many areas of el-Hibeh.

There is no end to the speculations one might make about the function of Building I. Perhaps these are foundations for a building whose upper portions have long since been looted for their bricks. As the space enclosed by the walls is quite small, and the wall pattern in TS1a is repeated almost exactly in TS1d, one might suspect that these walls formed a series of storage buildings—although these certainly would not be typical of the "granaries" found at el-Hibeh (Paribeni 1935).

In any case, soundly-based inferences about the shape and function of Building I will require additional excavations.

Once Building I's elements in TS1d had been revealed, mapped, and associated with their corresponding members in TS1a, they were removed. Over a hundred of the bricks were measured, and like those noted above, they showed extremely uniform size (ca. 39 x 18 x 12 cms).

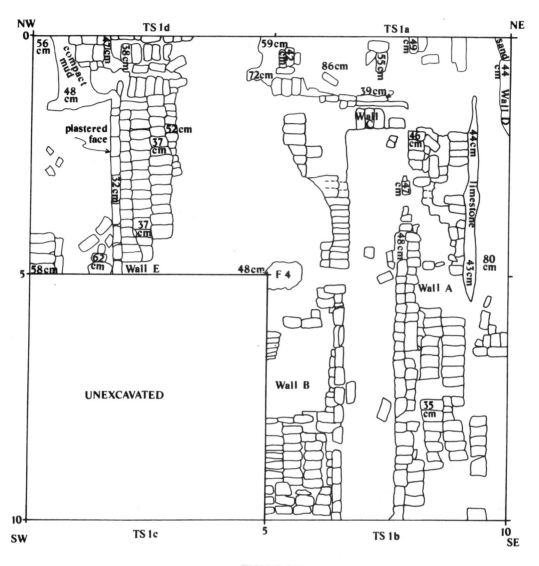

FIGURE 2.7
TS1a, TS1b, and TS1d, Building I

LEVEL 5a of TS1d encompassed the removal of the bricks to their bottom courses, and was so designated in order to keep separate the few sherds and other artifacts found in between and adjacent to these bricks.

LEVEL 5b involved the excavation of Feature 9, a circular area of ash, charcoal, and artifacts.

With excavation of LEVEL 6, we had removed Wall C of TS1d, and—as the season was nearing its end—we began the excavation of TS1b. Henceforth work at TS1b and TS1d proceeded concurrently.

As Figure 2.7 indicates, excavations of TS1b were quite limited: we removed the reed-debris overburden of Building I, revealing more of the length of this building's walls. Although numerous artifacts were recovered, architecturally speaking, TS1b added little to what we had determined on the basis of our work at TS1a and TS1d.

Fortunately, our excavations in the lower levels of TS1d were more informative. With the removal of Building I and excavations into Level 6 (Figure 2.8), a second building was revealed; a "T" shaped arrangement of walls constructed of somewhat smaller (ca. 30 x 20 x 10 cm) bricks. As Figure 2.8 indicates, Building II was associated with several pits and concentrations of artifacts. The building itself, unlike Building I, had a "classic" floor of hard-packed, finely laminated clays embedded with ash, charcoal, and tiny bits of flora and fauna. Feature 5, Lot 6 of Level 6 was a brick-lined pit containing considerable ash and other debris. Lot 3 contained two sharply defined ash concentrations, on the edges of which we found additional papyri fragments. The other lots excavated (Figure 2.8) as parts of Level 6 all contained the usual quantities of sherds, bones, fabrics, and other material.

With the excavation of LEVEL 6a, we began concentrating on the southeast corner of TS1d, in an effort to reach another building level before the season's end. At approximately 1.20 m depth in this area we encountered a brick-lined "fire-pit" (Feature 10, Figure 2.9) around which the sediments were exceptionally heavy with ash, charcoal, basketry fragments, sherds, bones (some of them calcined), and other debris. The plastered mud floor associated with this fire-pit seems to have been the same as that encountered in Lot 3 of TS1d though separated from it by Wall D. The floor near this fire-pit was somewhat thinner than that in Lots 3 and 4, and it may simply have been a compact area around an oven built against an outside wall of Building II.

Having taken various sediment and other samples from Lots 7 and 8 of TS1d, we removed the bricks lining this fire-pit.

Excavations in LEVEL 7 of TS1d involved removal of sediments from Lots 4, 6, 7, and 9.

LEVEL 8 of TS1d was excavated by removing additional sediments from Lots 4, 6, 7, and 9. Lot 9 contained some floor-like deposits of laminated clay layers, and at about 1.23 m depth in this lot another wall (Figure 2.9) was encountered in the southwest corner of the square. The single course of bricks preserved form only the outline of a wall. This was designated as Wall F and considered part of Building II, since Wall F is on the same level, is made of the same size bricks, and is directly perpendicular to Wall G of Building II.

One disconcerting aspect of Building II is that the walls in TS1a and TS1d did not align neatly. Also, while the walls of this level were only one course wide in TS1a, they were two to three courses wide in TS1d.

In the eastern part of Lot 9 of Level 8, we excavated a brick-lined pit (Feature 10) that was approximately 2.32 m deep (Figure 2.9). This was emptied in four arbitrary levels, each level containing sherds, bones, wood fragments, plant macrofossils, and other artifacts.

Excavation of LEVELS 10, 11, 12, and 13 were conducted only in the southern quarter of TS1d and involved mainly Lot 9 (Figure 2.10). Here, too, the objective was to reach another building level and gather additional stratified samples. At a depth of 1.96 m in this area we finally reached one wall (Wall A) of Building III (Figure 2.10) and took sediment samples near this construction. Unfortunately, we retrieved only a few sherds here (mainly in Feature 11, a mass of debris) and thus were not able to extend the seriation significantly.

FIGURE 2.8
TS1d, Level 6, Building II

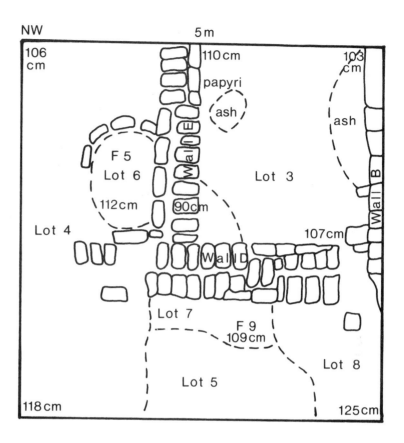

FIGURE 2.9
TS1d, Level 8, Building II

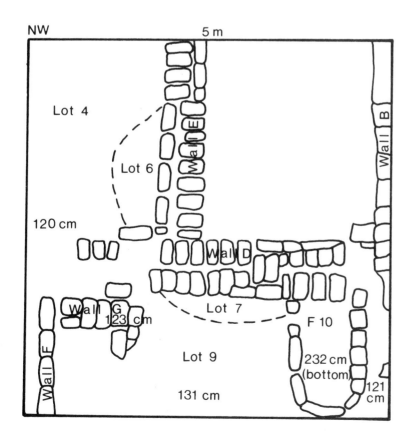

With the exposure of a small area of one wall of Building III, we reached the end of the season, insofar as Test Square 1 was concerned.

In summary of TS1, we defined three distinct superimposed building phases, each associated with numerous pits and other features. As indicated, the latest of these, Building I, seems to have been a non-residential structure of imposing size. Building II, although only partially exposed, is quite similar to the small mud-brick "houses" still standing in some areas of el-Hibeh. Very little can be said about Building III without additional excavation.

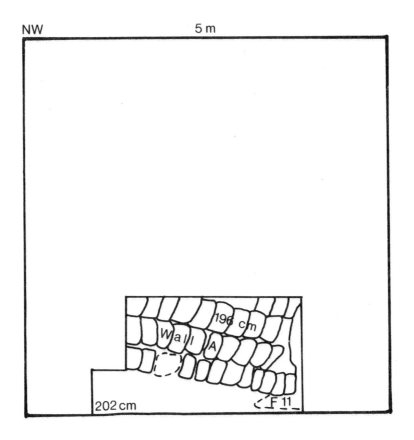

FIGURE 2.10
TS1d, Level 12, Building III

Test Square 2

Test Square 2 (TS2) was laid out to abut the enclosure wall and to encompass the brick architecture eroding from the surface (Figure 2.14). A sample of diagnostic sherds was taken from the square's surface.

About 5 cm of eroded deposits were removed as LEVEL 1 in the northwest quadrant, the surface of which was up to a meter higher than that of the two southern quadrants. The surface of TS2 was very uneven, sloping about 1 meter toward the southeast. Initial excavations were aimed at revealing more of the architecture and at defining cultural stratigraphy.

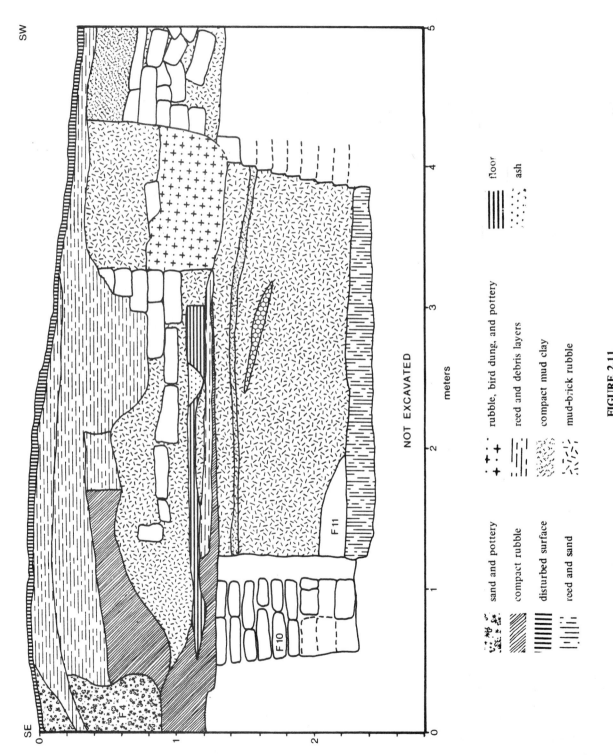

FIGURE 2.11
Test Square 1d, South Profile

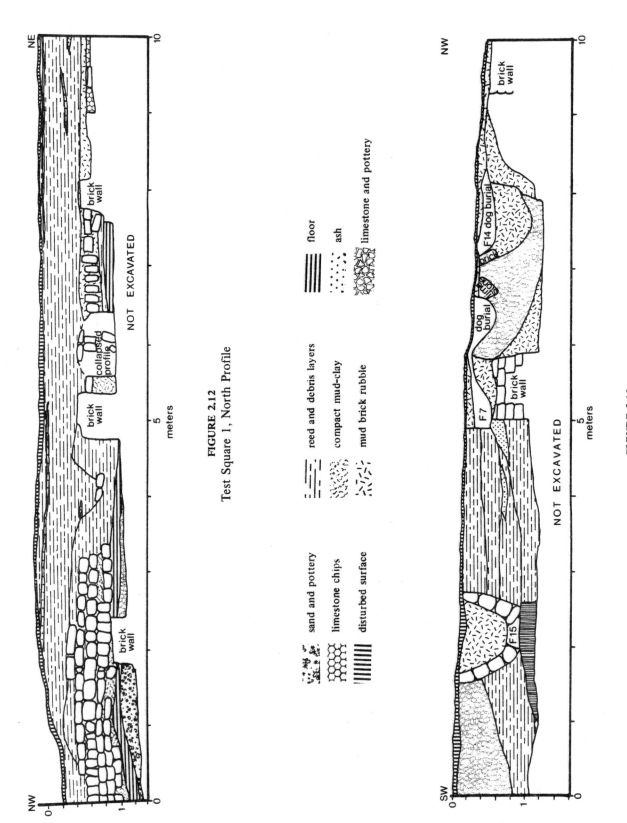

FIGURE 2.12
Test Square 1, North Profile

reed and debris layers

compact mud-clay

mud brick rubble

sand and pottery

limestone chips

disturbed surface

floor

ash

limestone and pottery

FIGURE 2.13
Test Square 2, West Profile

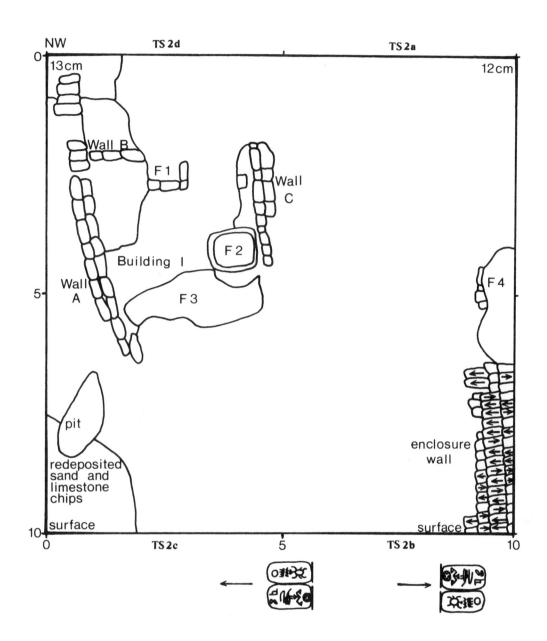

FIGURE 2.14
TS2, Level 2, Building I

The eroding brick architecture noted on the surface proved to be wall stubs of a structure, labelled "Building I," which was associated with two major features. Feature 1 was obviously a fire container of some kind, possibly a hearth. Heat had reddened the brick of which it was constructed, to a depth of 5 cm, and there was considerable ash in and around this feature. Feature 2 showed no evidence of firing, being composed of rather soft, heavily chaff-tempered, unfired mud. The contents were about 15 cm accumulation of unstratified sand, ash, and charcoal. The walls of Feature 2 were preserved only to a height of about 15 cm. It is likely this feature was a storage bin, most of which has been eroded. Feature 3 is a section of fill and floor—the only section of the floor associated with Building I that was largely intact. Fragments of cartouche-bearing bricks were found in the fill above this floor, along with large quantities of animal (sheep/goat) dung. Sediment samples were taken. The floor itself averaged about 5 cm thickness and was very well-defined, being composed of hard-packed reeds, dirt, and a limestone plaster. This floor, unfortunately, was not well-preserved in areas adjacent to the walls of Building I, but its elevation in areas where it was preserved was precisely what it should have been to intercept the wall. The floor did not extend west of Wall A of Building I (Figure 2.14).

Feature 4 is a dish-shaped pit comprising unstratified deposits of gray-brown silt with flecks of what appear to be limestone. There were few artifacts in this deposit and only one rim sherd. There seem to be two levels in this pit, the first about 6 cm thick, of silt with limestone flecks, the second about 11 cm, of similar appearance but somewhat harder and more compact. No significance is read into this distinction, and the area was labelled a feature only because it was of approximately human grave size and disarticulated human bones were found some 4 meters to the south.

Feature 5 was a pit (1.90 x .85 x .17 m depth) of clean fill, with bits of limestone and one pottery rim. Feature 6 was similar in contents, but extended to .65 m depth.

After Building I was drawn and photographed, it and its associated features were removed and their foundation levels excavated as LEVEL 2. Soil and artifact samples were taken and the majority of the fill inside the building and features was screened.

At this point the top 5 to 10 cm of TS2a and TS2c were removed as LEVEL 3, revealing the same reed-debris construction technique found in TS1 and elsewhere at el-Hibeh. It was apparent that interlocking sections of reed-debris layers were used as foundations for Building I. Excavations along the west baulk revealed Feature 7, a dog-burial. No grave goods were found with this animal, but it was surrounded by large bricks and brick fragments. Clearing should have revealed a distinct pit outline, but repeated examination under different kinds of light and with much cleaning suggests that pits cut into the eroded levels of the reed-debris constructions are not always visible.

Toward the bottom of LEVEL 3, it became apparent that Building I rested on a much more complex set of buildings (Building II, Figure 2.15), and we began the task of defining these constructions and collecting their contents in separate lots. Since the elements of Building II seemed parts of a single complex, we extended our excavation unit to the maximum 10 x 10 m size, encountering on the eastern side of the square more of the enclosure wall.

At just 20 cm depth, we found a beam (radiocarbon dated to 2756 B.P. ± 80 [Beta-Analytic, Libby Half-life, uncorrected]) plastered into a mud-brick wall (Wall E, Figure 2.15), which had approximately twelve evenly spaced holes (ca. 30 cm deep) on its eastern

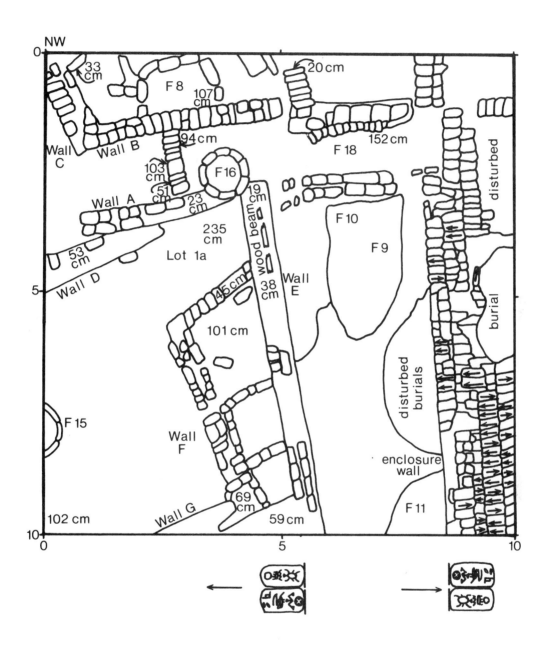

FIGURE 2.15
TS2, Level 6, Building II

face. This and other evidence led us to suspect that we had encountered the upper courses of a mud-brick structure that was preserved to a considerable height.

This interpretation was subsequently confirmed by the absence of floors or stratified occupational levels at any place within the excavation unit to a depth of over 2 meters. The fill around these walls and features was removed in 10 to 15 cm levels and the artifacts from these levels were kept separate. Most of the walls were almost perfectly preserved to a height of more than 2 meters, and only in a few areas did we reach their foundations.

Thus, the features, lots, and other designations of samples from TS2 refer almost exclusively to secondary deposits. The location of these was considered in the course of analyzing the ceramics and floral and faunal remains, but it is not appropriate to review their excavation history in detail here, since most of these samples come from refuse dumped in Building II after its abandonment. We have no way of determining at this point whether this in-filling took place in one or many episodes; perhaps Building II was filled to serve as a foundation for Building I.

One feature that is probably not attributable to in-filling is Feature 14, a second domestic dog burial. The fill enclosing this animal included brick fragments, but no grave goods of any kind.

In excavating TS2 we were intent upon recovering intact the deposits just above the floors of these various structures, so the pace of work was relatively slow, and it was near the end of the season before we emptied some areas of Building II.

Fragments of floors were encountered at 2.35 m depth in Lot 1a in the northeast area of Building II (Figure 2.15). Its composition—highly compacted small bits of rubble, a few sherds, charcoal, and organic material in laminated layers of a few centimeters each—is typical of a domestic residence. Approximately 46 cm below this floor, and separated from it by very compact reed-debris layers, was another floor, which abutted Wall E. This floor sloped slightly up at the point where it joined the wall and contained highly compacted clay, bones, charcoal, and other debris. The floor was (of course) reached on the planned last day of excavation, and although an additional day was spent excavating in this small area in order to recover pottery samples from levels underlying these buildings, the area it was possible to expose was so small that reliable samples of this earlier occupation could not be obtained. Sherds that were recovered were almost all body fragments of the shallow, sand-tempered orange bowls (Appendix 1, Types 116-117) found in great numbers in the foundations of the enclosure wall.

On the last day we tried to excavate to the bottom courses of the enclosure wall in the area to the east of Wall E, but its lowest levels were not reached, and, judging from the outside surface of the enclosure wall where looting has exposed its bottom course, excavations in TS2 would have had to continue for at least another 1.5 meters to reach these foundations.

As Table 3.1 indicates, the pottery found in all levels of TS2 is relatively similar, there being no indication that different depths are associated with different depositional events: it probably was filled in with deposits taken from a relatively early occupation of the site (note [Table 3.1] the lack of any pottery types like those associated with the last occupation at TS1). Type 116, which is found in large numbers in the foundations under the enclosure wall, is found throughout TS2 and in the deposits just under the floors on which most of the TS2 architecture stands, but although we know that this type was common in the 21st Dynasty occupations, we cannot conclude that it was in use during an earlier occupation of TS2.

Regarding the range of activities represented at TS2, Building I, with its fire pit and storage vessel, would seem best interpreted as a domestic residence.

Building II is much more complex architecturally and clearly involves at least some modifications over time. Speculations can be made about the use of the different structures, but there is little evidence with which to evaluate these speculations. The arrangement of the small units on the west side of Wall E, for example, may indicate a storage function. These units were too small for occupation, had no perceptible doors, and were formed by rather unstable, one-brick wide partition walls. No great quantities of chaff, stone, or other material survive to indicate what, if anything, was stored here, however.

Feature 18 (Figure 2.15), the vaulted structure in the northeast quarter of the unit, is located adjacent to the large, round storage bin (Feature 16), and both are contained in a small complex one might suspect was a granary of sorts. Analyses of the contents of these features (stored in the Egyptian musem) may help evaluate this possibility, but, like the rest of the unit, the refilling of these structures by redeposited occupational debris has removed much of the relevant evidence.

Perhaps the most that can be said of this unit is that the architecture is somewhat different from the usual domestic arrangement of living space, hearth, doorway, etc. The arrangement of the walls seems more suitable to a complex of utility buildings set between residential units and the enclosure wall. But the single-course interior walls, obvious storage bins, and other small constructions are certainly not inconsistent with the interpretation that these are remnants of a domestic or small-scale commercial economy.

III. RELATIVE SERIATION OF CERAMICS

In analyzing the el-Hibeh ceramics, we were particularly concerned with constructing a seriation of ceramic styles that would allow us to infer a relative chronology of these styles.

We encountered several problems in this regard. For example, the continual re-use of occupational debris as foundations for subsequent constructions mixed together ceramics of vastly different time and space proveniences. Also, there are few, if any, precisely excavated and analyzed samples of Late Period ceramics at other Middle Egyptian sites with which to compare the el-Hibeh materials.

Yet, as Table 3.1 illustrates, we were able to produce a persuasive seriation of ceramic types. In Table 3.1, the ceramics from thirty-four excavation units are expressed as frequencies of twenty-nine pottery "types." The excavation units have been arranged stratigraphically, so that the relative frequencies of pottery types in different levels can be directly compared.

The pottery types were constructed by the traditional method of separating individual rims, bases, decorated body sherds, and other "diagnostic" sherds into groups that had strong internal similarity in shape, size, temper, decoration, and other attributes. We attempted to assure some degree of comparability with other ceramic collections from elsewhere in Egypt by constructing types like those already established at other sites, but this was difficult to do without direct comparisons of the ceramics involved; and, most such existing types seem to have been created mainly for description—as opposed to seriation—purposes.

The ordering of the types in Table 3.1 was done with CLUSTAN (Wishart 1975), a set of computer programs involving numerical taxonomy, clustering, and other multivariate techniques. CLUSTAN's MODE and HIERARCHY subroutines were used to order the types in such a way that each ceramic type was placed adjacent to the type whose frequency in the various excavation units was most similar to its own. Since there are 29!/2 possible arrangements, however, this ordering must be considered approximate, in that there may be a "better" one, if one could examine all the possible permutations.

Ordering the ceramic types, rather than the excavations units, in this manner is somewhat unorthodox, but as Table 3.1 illustrates, these data do seem to fall into fairly neat patterns. One might, for example, hypothesize that there are three groups of contemporaneous types, consisting of Types 132 through Type 137 in group one, Types 201 through Type 138 in group two, and a third group consisting of Types 213 through 318. But it should be noted that several of the types (e.g., 311) are either present throughout the periods reflected in Table 3.1, or may be present in some units because of site disturbances. Other types, in contrast, (e.g., 132, 229, 127) seem to be quite time-sensitive and of limited use-period.

Table 3.1 is expressed in raw frequencies, rather than the traditional percentages,

TABLE 3.1

Stratigraphic Sequence of Frequencies of Selected Pottery Types from TS1 and TS2

Level Number	Lot Number	Bag Number	132	240	119	514	239	229	328	147	144	236	137	201	142	115	136	123	143	200	311	116	138	213	313	301	129	214	124	127	318
(TS-1)																														
1	1	209	9		1		1																								
2	1	207	1	1	1																										
3	1	254	1	1																											
3	1	256	1	1		3		4		4	2												1								
3	1	273	1					22			5						1														
3	1	268						6	8	4	1																				
3	2	277						6	1																						
4	1	274	1			1											1														
4	1	279	1	1	1			21			1	1	1									1									
4	1	282		1			4	27				2	1						1												
4	2	286						4				2																			
4	2	288						15				3																			
5	4	215								17	2																				
5	3	283						23				14																			
5	4	285				1		11				4	1																		
5	1	289						3				3																			
5	3	290										1			1									2					1		
5	1	292											2		1																
5a	4	300					1	6				1	6	1	1	1		1													
6	3	295										1	1																		
6	3	313										1	2		1			1	2												
6	4	319							2				2					1													
6	6	320							1			1	3	1	3			1	1	1		1	1								
6	8	329											2	2						2		1									
7	8	334											1		1				1												
7a	4	337													3	3						1									
10	9	348			1					1					2																
(TS-2)																															
1		530										10	6	13	9	11		6	4	6	2	2	2	3	4	5	1			2	
3/4		531										3	3	2	2			1			1		1	2	1	1					
F.13		549															1	1	1		1								1		
6		564										3	3		1	2		1	2	5	1				1					2	1
6		569										3	4	1	5	1		1	1	1	1			4	1				1	1	1
7		582										3	1	1	2	2		2	3	2	9			4		1			1	2	2
7		589										3	1	6	1	1			1	6	4	4	1	1	3	3	1			3	1
8		596										1								4	4	4	2	1	2	2	3	1	1	1	1

Pottery Types

because the pattern is essentially the same for frequencies and percentages, and the frequencies illustrate the relative sample sizes for the different types.

The apparent two- or three-part groupings of types in TS1 accord with a similar division of the stratigraphy of this unit (Figures 2.3 to 2.10) and support the interpretation (see above) of three distinct building phases at TS1. It is unfortunate, however, that few ceramics were found in the lowest levels of TS1, else the overlap between TS1 and TS2 may have been more apparent.

The lack of difference in type frequencies in different levels at TS2 is in agreement with our interpretation of the architecture of this unit: that it consists of one building phase only, and the filling-in of this building with debris was a short-term event.

Although the relative seriation of Table 3.1 appears to "work" in the sense that one can use these groups of types as relative time markers, this analysis raises several important questions about the general problem of seriating Egyptian artifacts.

First, although almost all archaeologists working in Egypt define ceramic types in essentially the same way we did at el-Hibeh, it should be recognized that these units violate one of the central assumptions of the relative seriation method, as it is commonly understood (Ford 1962; Dunnell 1970, 1981; Marquardt 1978): the seriation method assumes that the attributes on which a type is defined are *stylistic* in nature, and not in any way an expression of *functional* variability. Thus, the frequency of that type in a sample must be assumed to vary only with the passage of time, not with a change in the types of activities performed. Obviously, any types based (as the el-Hibeh types are) on vessel size, wall thickness, temper, or gross shape may well have more to do with what kinds of things were being done at a site than with changing styles of artifacts at that site. At el-Hibeh, for example, we have no way of knowing with certainty whether Type 301 (a form of round base) occurs in TS2 but not in TS1 because TS2 is earlier in time than TS1 or because activities involving large round-based vessels were conducted at TS2 but not at TS1.

Most ceramic types like these are probably so highly "loaded" with stylistic variability that they work well as "index fossils" (Adams 1965:121), and in most areas of the world their usefulness in chronological seriation has been confirmed through excavations. But it must be assumed that units defined partly in terms of size, vessel shape, and other such characteristics vary to some degree in response to functional factors. And if so, it seems obvious that more powerful analytical units could be constructed if stylistic and functional variability were separated.

Several methods have been proposed to partition stylistic and functional variability. Dunnell (1970:307, 1981) has argued that the proper units for chronological seriation should be paradigmatically defined classes created through intentional definitions, and that these units should be tested against the assumptions of the seriation method (e.g., that the units are of equivalent duration in time, with unimodal and continuous distributions through time, etc.) before being used in relative seriations. He specifically rejects in this context the units produced by numerical taxonomic methods.

A different approach to the problem of partitioning functional and stylistic variability has been taken by Marquardt (1978), Benfer (1975), Drennan (1976), Close (1980), and others who have used multivariate statistics of attribute combinations to "factor out" stylistic and functional variability.

But since there are no demonstrated *explanations* of stylistic behavior (only empirical generalizations, like the "gravity model" [Marquardt 1978]), we lack any absolutely certain way of defining and measuring stylistic behavior, or of choosing between methods to partition stylistic and functional variability.

Another difficulty, one that is particularly severe in Egypt, is that the seriation method is based on the assumption that stylistic variability over *space* can be controlled. Thus, the most effective relative seriations can be conducted only for small areas where there is substantial exchange among the communities, so that styles are well "mixed" and one can then assume that the frequency of a stylistic element at a given site is unrelated to the distance from that site to the other sites in the area for which the relative seriation is being constructed (Deetz and Dethlefsen 1965).

But in Egypt, transport of ceramics on the Nile has a long history, and the linear arrangement of settlements along the river's banks tends to distort the usual "gravity model" distribution of stylistic elements (Binford and Binford 1966:240). In the absence of evidence to the contrary, one must at least consider the possibility that any particular style of pottery was distributed in Egyptian settlements in part on the basis of administrative systems linking major communities. If so, a particular style may be present at a large site, but absent at smaller sites, because of differences in their administrative roles—not because of differences in their periods of occupation.

As noted, despite all these difficulties, Egyptian pottery typologies seem to work well enough for purposes of relative chronological seriation that we might question the relevance of recent, highly statistical work on the seriation problem (see especially Cowgill, Whallon, and Ottaway 1981).

But archaeologists working in Egypt can take advantage of this recent theoretical work on the seriation problem in several ways. For example, most coding and cataloguing systems of Egyptian ceramics are object-based rather than attribute-based, and blend in many kinds of stylistic and mechanical attributes. The studies referenced above suggest that for purposes of relative seriation, it would be more useful to concentrate typological work on attribute combinations, so that these combinations rather than the individual sherds become the units of analysis. Mass-production of the later Egyptian ceramics insures that attribute combinations "correlate" well with individual sherds, but more precise seriations could probably be produced through attribute analysis.

These attribute combinations must then be tested against the assumptions of the seriation method, and typological distinctions that do not accord with the model should be eliminated as elements in the seriation.

A more fundamental issue involves the *purposes* for which Egyptian artifact types are created. It is a fundamental assumption of science that one's theory determines the analytical units one creates and uses. In Egyptian archaeology the primary objective in pottery typologies seems to have been the creation of essential *descriptive* types of the polythetic-agglomerative kinds (Doran and Hodson 1975), which were subsequently and inappropriately used for not only chronological seriations, but functional seriations, reconstructions of trade patterns, and art historical analyses as well.

It is difficult to imagine that such units can be of much analytical importance, but if they remain valued for their descriptive uses, they probably should be constructed on a paradigmatic basis rather than on the traditional numerical taxonomic basis. That is, dimensions of variability should be defined (e.g., color, temper, etc.), and each sherd scored on those dimensions, which are infinitely extendable and infinite in number. Thus, any sherd could be compared directly to any other sherd and the addition of new samples would not change the basic types employed. As presently constituted, the traditional Egyptian pottery types are less than perfect units, either for constructing relative seriations or simply for comparing the ceramics from one site with those of another.

I hope to pursue some of these issues in subsequent work on the el-Hibeh materials and other data (Wenke and Lane, eds. n.d.).

In the meantime, Table 3.1 should be understood merely as a preliminary definition of the forms of ceramic variability that may be useful in inferring a relative chronology of el-Hibeh's occupations.

Having presented a description of basic archaeological methods and results, let us consider at this point other categories of evidence bearing on el-Hibeh's history and significance.

As is discussed below, based on the relative seriation and other data, the time covered by the deposits in TS1 and TS2 probably extends from about 1000 B.C. to about A.D. 400.

IV. THE FAUNAL REMAINS

RICHARD REDDING

University of Michigan, Ann Arbor

Several faunal reports, either preliminary or final, are available for samples of bones from sites representing the Late Paleolithic, Neolithic, and Predynastic periods in Egypt. In contrast to the coverage of these periods, the fauna associated with dynastic and later periods are poorly documented. The faunal data published for the dynastic and later periods consist mainly of reports on individual specimens recovered from tombs (e.g., the Apis Bull by Duerst [1926]; goats by Pia [1942]; pigs by Staffe [1938]; and dogs by Gaillard and Daressy [1905], and Hutchinson [1962]) or on interpretations of reliefs and hieroglyphs by Zeuner (1963), Epstein (1971), and many others. Complete faunal reports of excavated material for the dynastic and later periods are rare; hence, the faunal remains from el-Hibeh, dating to the Late and Ptolemaic Periods, are of importance.

Unfortunately, this report must be considered as preliminary because only the mammalian remains have been examined in detail and only those from one of the two excavation units are completed. The description of the remains in this report is based primarily on the material from the twelve levels in Test Square 1 (TS1), supplemented by evidence from the partially completed analysis of the faunal materials from Test Square 2.

Faunal samples were recovered by screening all primary deposits through sieves of approximately 4 x 4 mm mesh size, and by individual recovery during the excavation process.

A. The Material

The excavations at TS1 yielded 565 bone fragments (weighing 3590.5 grams) that could be identified as mollusc, fish, reptile, bird, or mammal. An additional small quantity of bone was totally unidentifiable. When the bones from TS2 are completely analyzed, I expect the total count and weight of bone for el-Hibeh to more than double these TS1 figures.

Molluscs

The phylum Mollusca is represented in the TS1 sample by thirty-nine fragments weighing 95.6 gm. The final identifications have not been made, but one fragment is from a *Mutela* sp., one from a *Lanistes carinatus*, one from a *Viviparus unicolor*, and two from *Anisus planorbis*. Most (thirty-three) of the remaining shell fragments are either unidentifiable or represent a unionid. The single remaining fragment represents a marine mollusc of the family Cypraeidae, a cowrie.

The only mollusc likely to have been consumed as a regular part of the diet is the unionid, but there is no direct evidence of such consumption. A summary of counts and weights of molluscs for each level in TS1 is presented in Table 4.1.

Fish

The class Osteichthyes is represented in the TS1 sample by eighty-one fragments weighing 94.1 gm. None of the material has been identified in detail, but at least two catfish and one non-catfish species are present in the sample. The material consists primarily of elements of the head and pectoral girdle; vertebrae appear to be under-represented.

Although none of the fragments exhibited butchering marks and only two were affected by fire, fish were almost certainly part of the diet. The under-representation of vertebrae may be due to the differential treatment of these elements in the processing of fish—vertebrae were the only fish bone to show the effect of fire. A summary of counts and weights of fish remains by level for TS1 is presented in Table 4.1.

Turtle

Two carapace fragments, weighing 14.5 gm, represent the soft-shelled turtle, *Trionyx triunguis*. Neither fragment exhibits butchering marks or the effect of fire. However, Churcher (1972:26) states that the soft-shelled turtle has long been considered a delicacy by the peoples of the Nile Valley; hence, these two fragments probably represent animals consumed by the inhabitants of el-Hibeh. The distribution of turtle remains in TS1 is presented in Table 4.1.

Bird

The class Aves is represented at TS1 by only three fragments (total weight is 4.7 gm), which have not yet been identified. Bird bones are more numerous in TS2 and appear to be from larger taxa than those in TS1. Although the fragments do not exhibit any signs of butchering or burning, we can postulate that birds were consumed, since the elements identified are pigeon, the common crane, and the Egyptian goose, all of which are known historically to have been aviary-kept birds. A summary of counts and weights of bird remains by level for TS1 is presented in Table 4.1.

Mammals

The class Mammalia is represented in the TS1 sample by 448 fragments that weighed 3381.6 gm. Of this total, eighty-two fragments (weighing 1747.5 gm) were identifiable to at least the level of the genus. The distribution of these identifiable elements by taxa and level is presented in Table 4.2. Another 232 fragments (weighing 1494.5 gm) were classed as large or medium mammal and, within each of these classes, as either a limb, rib, vertebra, tooth, or skull fragment. The distribution among the classes and by level of these 232 fragments is presented in Table 4.3. The remaining 134 fragments (weighing 140.6 gm) are identifiable only as mammal.

Several of the seventy-nine identifiable elements were complete enough to permit one or more measurements to be taken. The system used for taking and labeling the measurements is described by Von Den Driesch (1976). A measurement followed by a plus sign (+) indicates that the measure may be an underestimate because of the loss of cortical bone due to erosion. A measurement followed by an "e" indicates that the measure is only an estimate because corners have been broken.

CROCIDURA FLAVESCENS. A maxilla with the premolar and two unicuspids, weighing 0.04 gm, was identified as the Giant Musk Shrew. This specimen came from Level 12 of TS1. This shrew is common at present in Lower Egypt, inhabiting canal banks and cultivated fields (Osborn and Helmy 1980:76). Since there is no indication that the Giant Musk Shrew was exploited as a food item, its presence at the site can probably be attributed to natural causes (e.g., it may have died on the site, or it may have been carried onto the site by a cat or raptor).

CANIS sp. Six elements, weighing 5.9 gm, were identifiable as *Canis* sp. Based on size, these elements represent a medium-sized dog or jackal, animals that probably were not eaten by humans. A distal metapodial had a breadth (Bd) of 8.14 mm.

EQUUS ASINUS. The ass is represented by eighteen fragments weighing 515.0 gm. The material from TS1 is exclusively teeth and distal limb elements (i.e., podials, metapodials, and phalanges), but proximal limb elements were recovered in TS2. Measurements taken on the elements are presented in Table 4.4. Measurements from a complete metacarpal with a length of 203 mm and a minimum width of the diaphysis of 26.5 mm were used to calculate a length-width index, as suggested by Hilzheimer (1941:10-14), resulting in a value of 13.0, which compares well with the range of values Hilzheimer provides for the ass, *E. asinus*. Boessneck's (1976:23) complete ass metacarpal from Tell el-Dab'a (dating to between 1750 and 1550 B.C.) is smaller than one from el-Hibeh, (greatest length [GL] 179.5 mm versus 203 mm), but the length-width indexes are almost identical, 13.0 for the el-Hibeh metacarpal and 13.1 for the el-Dab'a metacarpal. The greatest length measures for the two el-Hibeh first phalanges, 70.92 and 71-72e mm, are in the high end of the range, 60 to 72 mm, published by Boessneck (1976:24) for the first phalanges from Tell el-Dab'a. The distal tibia from TS2 has a greater breadth and depth than a distal tibia from Tell el-Dab'a, BD 58.72 versus 47 mm, and Dd 37 versus 31.54 mm.

Wild asses were consumed in the Late Paleolithic (Churcher 1972) and in the Neolithic (Redding n.d.), but it is unlikely that domestic asses would have been consumed in the Late or Ptolemaic periods, and none of the el-Hibeh equid material exhibited any signs of butchering or burning. This is in contrast to material from the other large mammal at el-Hibeh, cattle, which was certainly eaten and several examples of which from TS1 and TS2 exhibited butchering marks.

SUS SCROFA. The pig is represented by six fragments weighing 120.6 gm. The measurements for an atlas and two teeth are presented in Table 4.5. Also in Table 4.5 are measurements for a maxilla with four teeth, including an M^3, recovered from TS2. The length of the M^3, 28.75 mm, places it in the range of the domestic pig, which was a common domesticate in Egypt in the dynastic periods (Epstein 1971:340-45).

Although none of the pig bones from TS1 exhibits any signs of burning or butchering, the sample is small and all of the elements are from the head (a fact interesting in itself). It seems likely that domestic pigs were kept and eaten at el-Hibeh.

OVIS-CAPRA. Sheep-goats are represented by twelve fragments weighing 124.7 gm. The measurements for two mandibles, loose teeth, and a scapula are presented in Table 4.6, and they are in the range or slightly larger than those for similar elements from Tell el-Dab'a (Boessneck 1976:29). None of the sheep-goat bones from TS1 or TS2 can be positively identified as sheep as opposed to goat, or vice versa, but a horn (*Cornua*) from TS1, which is not included in the bone counts, is from a sheep.

Sheep-goats were certainly consumed and were probably milked and shorn also. Although none of the elements from TS1 provides any evidence of burning or butchering, an atlas from TS2 has several butchering marks.

BOS TAURUS. Domestic cattle are represented by thirty-four fragments weighing 963.9 gm. The measurements taken on four elements are presented in Table 4.7. Boessneck (1976:27) gives 74 mm as the greatest length lateral (GL1) for an astragalus from Tell el-Dab'a, and an identical value was obtained for the same measurement for an astragalus from TS1.

Cattle were certainly consumed at el-Hibeh and may also have been milked. Four cattle elements from TS1 and TS2 exhibit butchering marks.

The cattle raised in Egypt at present are the short-horned form, *Bos taurus brachyceros*, while the earliest domestic cattle in Egypt were the long-horned form, *Bos taurus primigenius* (Epstein 1971:213-26). Epstein (1971:288) suggests that the short-horned form first appeared in Egypt about the middle of the third millennium B.C. and became the dominant breed during the Hyksos period. Howard (1962) has suggested that the replacement of the long-horned form by *B. t. brachyceros* is related to the increased utilization of milk and dairy products: short-horned breeds being more efficient milk producers. While the sample of cattle from el-Hibeh is small, it is from this and similar sites that data will come to test this hypothesis and to examine the dynamics of the shift.

GAZELLA sp. Three elements weighing 16.4 gm represent a gazelle species. Gazelle meat is a delicacy in the Middle East, and gazelle were probably killed and consumed whenever possible.

MUS MUSCULUS. A mandible, with incisor, of the house mouse was recovered from LEVEL 6 of TS1. The house mouse occurs in Egypt at present, where it is found in fields, gardens, granaries, and houses (Osborn and Helmy 1980:283).

LEPUS CAPENSIS. The cape hare is represented by a scapula fragment, weighing 0.5 gm, recovered from LEVEL 12 at TS1. Hares are found in a variety of habitats in Egypt at present (Osborn and Helmy 1980:90), and although they were eaten at el-Hibeh, they probably did not make a major contribution to the diet of its inhabitants.

ADDITIONAL TAXA FROM TS2. Two taxa have been encountered in the sample from TS2 that were not found in the TS1 material. A PM^3 from a lion, *Felis leo*, was recovered from LEVEL 7 at TS2. A radius of the Bubal Hartebeest, *Alcelaphus buselaphus*, was recovered from LEVEL 8 of TS2. The proximal breadth (Bp) of this radius is 57.03 mm and the breadth of the Facies articularis proximalis (Bfp) is 52.60 mm.

B. Relative Importance of the Taxa and Associations

In the TS1 sample, fish are the most important non-mammalian resource. However, as the ratio of mammalian to non-mammalian remains demonstrates (17.2:1 by weight), the contribution of non-mammalian taxa to the diet of the inhabitants of el-Hibeh is minimal.

Species ratios, based on total bone weight, illustrating the relative importance of each of the mammalian taxa are presented in Table 4.8. Cattle dominate the mammalian sample with ass second in importance. Pig elements are slightly more common than sheep-goat material, and gazelle bones are least common among the major mammalian taxa. Of greatest interest are the relationships between cattle, sheep-goats, and pigs, which are the major meat-producing taxa. Although cattle bones weigh more than those of sheep, goats, and pigs, cattle provide much more meat; hence, the dominance of cattle apparent in the bone weights is probably real. Cattle and sheep-goats were probably utilized for products other than meat, but in contribution of meat to the diet of the inhabitants of el-Hibeh, cattle are much more important—at least in this extremely small sample. Sheep-goats and pigs appear to have contributed about equally to the diet in terms of meat, but sheep-goats probably also contributed milk.

The dominance of the mammalian sample by large mammals, which is apparent in the identifiable material, (a ratio of large to medium mammal by weight of 5.6:1–3.7:1 if the equid material is not added to the large mammal total), is supported by the unidentifiable mammalian material. The ratio of weight of unidentifiable large mammal bone to unidentifiable medium mammal bone is 5.6:1.

C. Conclusions

Probably the most important statement to be made regarding el-Hibeh fauna is that all conclusions based on the material recovered in the excavations must be viewed with caution for three reasons. First, the sample is extremely small. A larger sample from similar cultural contexts might result in different interpretations. Second, only the bone from TS1 is utilized in the analysis, so much of the bone probably comes from a limited range of cultural contexts. Samples from other cultural contexts might provide different results. Third, the analysis of the material is not yet complete.

With these *caveats* in mind, the major conclusions that can be drawn from the TS1 faunal data are:

1) Fish contributed more to the diet than any other non-mammalian taxon.
2) Non-mammalian taxa did not contribute much meat, by volume, to the diet.
3) Cattle were more important contributors of meat to the diet than were sheep-goats or pigs.

4) Pigs and sheep-goats were of about equal importance in terms of contribution of meat to the diet.

5) Wild mammals, hartebeest, and gazelle were still hunted.

When analysis of the TS2 fauna is completed, these generalizations will be reassessed to see if they are still applicable to the el-Hibeh fauna.

TABLE 4.1

**Weights in Grams (and Counts) of
Non-Mammalian Remains by Taxa, Unit, and Level for TS-1**

UNIT	LEVEL	SHELL	FISH	TURTLE	BIRD
TS-1b	1	14.0(8)	3.9(4)	-	-
	3	17.4(3)	1.7(2)	-	-
	4	-	-	-	-
	5	2.5(1)	25.1(3)	-	4.1(2)
	6	-	15.3(22)	-	-
	7	3.5(2)	15.3(22)	-	-
TS-1d	3	26.9(7)	6.0(4)	5.7(1)	-
	4	-	-	-	0.6(1)
	5	10.1(10)	10.8(25)	8.8(1)	-
	6	0.5(2)	8.7(9)	-	-
	7	-	-	-	-
	8	5.7(1)	-	-	-
	10	14.1(4)	18.6(8)	-	-
	12	0.9(1)	40.0(4)	-	-
TOTALS		95.6(39)	94.1(81)	14.5(2)	4.7(3)

TABLE 4.2

Weights in Grams (and Counts) of
Identified Mammal by Taxa, Unit, and Level for TS-l *

UNIT	LEVEL	CANIS SP.	EQUUS	SUS	BOS	OVIS-CAPRA	GAZELLA	TOTALS
TS-lb	1	-	42.8(2)	-	42.9(15)	-	-	92.0(17)
	3	-	25.2(1)	-	83.9(3)	-	-	109.1(4)
	4	-	-	-	52.9(1)	-	-	52.9(1)
	5	-	-	-	-	-	-	-
	6	-	-	-	38.6(1)	0.4(1)	-	39.0(2)
	7	-	-	22.8(2)	22.4(2)	66.5(7)	3.6(1)	115.3(12)
TS-1d	3	5.9(6)	296.0(9)	0.6(1)	63.6(2)	20.1(2)	-	386.2(20)
	4	-	116.7(4)	-	-	-	-	116.7(4)
	5	-	-	-	91.2(4)	-	-	91.2(4)
	6	-	34.3(2)	-	159.1(2)	15.1(1)	-	208.5(5)
	7	-	-	-	85.7(1)	-	12.8(2)	98.5(3)
	8	-	-	-	288.6(2)	-	-	288.6(2)
	10	-	-	97.2(3)	28.7(1)	-	-	125.9(4)
	12	-	-	-	-	22.6(1)	-	22.6(1)
TOTALS		5.9 (6)	515.0 (18)	120.6 (6)	963.9 (34)	124.7 (12)	16.4 (3)	1746.5 (79)

*To obtain the weight and count totals cited in the text, the weights and counts for *Crocidura flavescens, Mus musculus,* and *Lepus capensis* must be added to the totals in this table.

TABLE 4.3
Weights in Grams (and Counts) of Unidentified Mammalian Material by Element Type, Unit, and Level for TS-1

UNIT	LEVEL	MEDIUM MAMMAL						LARGE MAMMAL						TOTAL
		limb	rib	vert.	teeth	skull	total	limb	rib	vert.	teeth	skull	total	
TS-1b	1	31.1 (7)	-	-	3.5 (6)	-	34.6 (13)	65.8 (6)	7.3 (1)	-	-	-	73.1 (7)	107.7 (20)
	3	4.3 (3)	-	-	-	-	4.3 (3)	94.3 (9)	20.4 (2)	71.9 (4)	-	-	186.6 (15)	109.9 (18)
	4	-	-	-	-	-	-	-	23.8 (3)	-	-	-	23.8 (3)	23.8 (3)
	5	-	-	-	-	-	-	-	10.4 (1)	6.9 (1)	-	-	17.3 (2)	17.3 (2)
	6	0.9 (1)	-	-	-	-	0.9 (1)	66.6 (2)	-	-	-	-	66.6 (2)	67.5 (3)
	7	22.8 (3)	9.4 (3)	-	-	-	32.2 (6)	-	-	-	-	-	-	32.2 (6)
TS-1d	3	6.3 (7)	2.0 (1)	-	1.1 (3)	16.5 (6)	25.9 (17)	168.7 (16)	53.3 (2)	-	-	3.3 (1)	225.3 (19)	251.2 (36)
	4	6.8 (3)	11.3 (2)	-	1.5 (5)	-	19.6 (10)	29.1 (4)	-	-	-	-	29.1 (4)	48.7 (14)
	5	43.1 (24)	9.2 (3)	-	12.1 (7)	-	64.5 (34)	292.9 (45)	60.1 (4)	59.5 (5)	2.4 (1)	11.9 (1)	426.8 (56)	491.3 (90)
	6	8.4 (9)	0.4 (2)	-	-	4.1 (1)	12.9 (12)	54.8 (6)	27.1 (1)	24.3 (2)	-	-	106.2 (9)	119.1 (21)
	7	-	-	-	0.8 (1)	-	0.8 (1)	-	-	-	-	-	-	0.8 (1)
	8	-	-	-	-	-	-	-	-	-	-	-	-	- (1)
	10	8.4 (2)	-	-	-	-	8.4 (2)	-	-	-	-	-	-	8.4 (2)
	12	12.7 (7)	10.7 (1)	-	-	-	23.4 (8)	97.2 (6)	2.8 (1)	12.2 (1)	-	-	112.2 (8)	135.6 (16)
TOTALS		144.8 (66)	43.0 (12)	-	19.1 (22)	20.6 (7)	227.5 (107)	893.2 (97)	181.4 (12)	174.8 (13)	2.4 (1)	15.2 (2)	1267.0 (125)	1494.5 (232)

TABLE 4.4

Measurements of Equid Remains from TS1

ELEMENT	MEASUREMENTS (mm)		
PM^2	B −q	L 24.97	
M$^{1\text{-}2}$	B 26.00	L 24.25	
	B 26.66	L -	
M$_{1\text{-}2}$	B 15.00	L 22.64	
M$_3$	B 11.10	L 24.34	
Metacarpal	Bp 43.21	Bd 39.00	SD 26.50
	GL 203	GL1 201	LI 196
Metatarsal	Bp 39.16		
First Phalanx	GL 70.72		
	GL 71-72e[1]		
Scapula (from TS-2)	GLp 64.90	Lg 47.05+[2]	
Tibia (from TS-2)	Bd 58.72	Dd 31.54	

ABBREVIATIONS:

B breadth	L length	G (in first position) greatest
G (in second position) glenoid	D diameter	H height
Fcr facies articularis cranialis	Fcd facies articularis caudalis	l lateral
d distal	p proximal	

[1] A measurement followed by an "e" indicates that the specimen was broken and the measurement is an estimate.

[2] A measurement followed by a plus (+) indicates that the specimen has lost cortical bone to erosion and the measurement on the specimen when in a fresh condition would have been slightly larger.

TABLE 4.5

Measurements of Pig Remains from TS1

ELEMENT	MEASUREMENTS (mm)		
Atlas	BFcr 53.60 BFcd 47.86	H 37.89	GB 75.41
M^1	B 13.76	L 16.38	
M^2	B 15.30	L 19.11	
Maxilla (from TS2)			
PM^4	B 12.32	L 12.03	
M^1	B –	–	
M^2	B 17.22	L 20.81	
M^3	B 18.54	L 18.75	

TABLE 4.6

Measurements of Sheep-Goat Remains from TS1

ELEMENT	MEASUREMENTS (mm)	
PM^4	B 6.45	L 11.90

Mandible

Length from Gonion caudale to aboral border of the aveolus of the M_3	49.05
Length from Gonion caudale to oral border of the aveolus of the PM_2	118.69
Length from Gonion caudale to the most aboral indentation of the mental foramen	129.86
Length of the cheektooth row	70.14
Length of the molar row	46.44
Length of the premolar row	24.00
Length of the diastema	38.69
Aboral height of the vertical ramus	66.97
Height of the mandible behind the M_3	28.98
Height of the mandible in front of the M_1	20.82
Height of the mandible in front of the PM_2	16.00+

M_1	B 7.98	L 10.00e
M_2	B 8.77	L 13.00e
M_3	B 9.08	L 22.52
Scapula	GLp 34.78	BG 20.93

TABLE 4.7

Measurements of Cattle Remains from TS1

ELEMENT	MEASUREMENTS (mm)	
Metacarpal	Dp	36.09
Metacarpal	SD	36.31
Astragalus	GL1	74.00+
Central + 4th Tarsal	GB	59.67
Central + 4th Tarsal	GB	60.96

TABLE 4.8

Species Ratios, Based on Weight, Illustrating The Relative Importance of the Mammalian Taxa

Bos	58.7	7.7	8.0	1.9
Equus	31.4	4.1	4.3	-
Sus	7.3	0.97	-	-
Ovis-Capra	7.6	-	-	-
	Gazella	*Ovis-Capra*	*Sus*	*Equus*

V. THE PLANT REMAINS

WILMA WETTERSTROM*
Massachusetts Institute of Technology, Cambridge

The archaeological plant remains from the site of el-Hibeh, spanning the 1st millennium B.C., offer a rare opportunity to trace the evolution of foods and farming practices during an extremely turbulent period of Egyptian history. The plant remains dating from the 21st Dynasty and the Persian invasion should offer insights into how the upheavals of these periods disrupted agriculture. For example, the floral remains might reflect neglected irrigation systems or changes in cropping patterns. Likewise, the materials from the later Ptolemaic period might indicate how well the new conquerors succeeded in controlling agriculture and increasing crop productivity. The Ptolemaic plant remains should also be a valuable complement to the documentary sources from this period as well as a check on them.

A small preliminary study of the el-Hibeh plant remains, recently undertaken, focused on two issues: gaining some insight into el-Hibeh's plant economy and assessing the site's potential for research on agricultural evolution in Egypt. The sample, consisting mainly of large items picked by hand, was too limited to offer any definitive conclusions. But despite the sample size, the collection proved to be surprisingly rich and demonstrated that plant remains are abundant and well-preserved at el-Hibeh. The sample, reflecting the wealth of the Nile Valley, documents most of the major crops of Pharaonic Egypt including emmer wheat, barley, and flax, a wide variety of fruits, as well as common field weeds. In addition, the sample shows evidence of the new crops the Ptolemies introduced to Egypt including naked wheat, olives, and peaches.

A. Methods

During the 1980 work at el-Hibeh two 10 x 10 meter test squares were excavated, as allowed by the terms of the permit from the Egyptian Antiquities Service. Plant remains were systematically collected from both units in three ways:

1) All specimens encountered during excavation were removed by hand. These consisted of relatively large, obvious items such as peach stones and date pits.
2) Smaller items were caught in a 4 x 4 mm mesh sieve through which all of the deposits were screened.
3) Sediment samples, presumably containing plant remains, were collected and bagged to be fine-sieved or floated at a later date. It was hoped that these bags, collected systematically with a uniform volume, would yield a representative and reliable

*Present address: Botanical Museum, Harvard University, Cambridge.

sample of the plant remains at the site including the smallest size classes of macroscopic specimens.

Unfortunately, the preliminary analysis of the plant remains, conducted at MIT, had to be
limited to the first two sets of material. The bags of sediments, and floral remains from
TS1d, which are still in the Egyptian Museum in Cairo, could not be shipped to the United
States. As a result the collection studied is biased for large, visible items. However, this
limitation was partially overcome with a third set of materials found "hitchhiking" in the
sample bags. Consisting of small items, these specimens were apparently in the sediments
adhering to the larger hand-picked plant remains when they were bagged in the field. When
the larger samples were unpacked at MIT the sediments in the specimen bags were carefully
collected and systematically scanned for small seeds and other plant parts.

As a result of these procedures the collection must be viewed as two very different
types of samples. The large, hand-picked or screened specimens, systematically collected,
represent virtually all of the large, obvious floral materials in the two test squares. They are
probably a good indication of the types and relative proportions of large items preserved
here. The smaller specimens, on the other hand, inadvertently picked up, are a haphazard,
chance assortment. The size of the sediment samples included with the larger plant remains
ranged widely, while the number of these samples collected in each excavation unit varied.
As a result the small specimens cannot necessarily be considered representative of all the
types and the frequency of smaller materials preserved here. However, they offer valuable
insights into the kind of remains, the relative quantities preserved, and their state of preservation.

In the laboratory both sets of materials were examined with the naked eye and where
necessary with a binocular dissecting microscope at low power magnification. Specimens
were identified on the basis of morphological features carefully compared with those
of modern and archaeological reference materials. Measurements were made with a cali-
pers. However, the wood specimens, which are a part of this collection, have not yet been
analyzed.

B. Results

Test Squares 1 and 2 at el-Hibeh produced a large quantity of plant remains—over 1000
individual items from TS1, which dates from Ptolemaic times, and nearly 800 items from
TS2, which is earlier. Most of the materials are desiccated and well-preserved. They retain
most of their original morphological features and some of the seed coats are even glossy. Of
course, the sample shows an obvious bias for hard, imperishable substances such as the stony
sclereid cells of fruit stones, or the tough cellulose of stems, or the hard, waxy walls of seed
coats. The less durable portions of the plants, such as the embryos and starchy endosperms
of seeds, have suffered considerably. For example, in nearly all of the seeds the embryos are
completely gone, and much of the endosperm has decomposed. It is not surprising that the
collection includes little evidence of soft, fleshy items with a high moisture content, such as
leafy greens.

The collection also shows a strong bias for waste products—the inedible and unusuable
portions of a plant, such as fruit stones or grain stems. This is not surprising since all of the

specimens were recovered among debris. As a result, the el-Hibeh plant remains present an interesting contrast to the majority of plant collections from Egypt which have come from tombs. The el-Hibeh materials probably reflect more accurately the Egyptian crop economy than the tomb offerings do. For example, the latter probably include only the best specimens and perhaps only traditional foods, while the household trash samples should reflect most of the plants used in the community and should include the poorer specimens.

As a cross-section of the crop economy, the el-Hibeh materials reflect mainly field and orchard crops, along with weed seeds. Nearly all of these were grown in Egypt and probably were cultivated near el-Hibeh. They include the following, listed in order of abundance by class:

CEREALS: Emmer wheat (*Triticum dicoccum*)
                    Barley, 6-row, hulled (*Hordeum vulgare*)
                    Naked wheat, probably durum (*Triticum* cf. *durum*)

OIL PLANTS: Olive (*Olea europaea*)
                    Flax (*Linum usitatissimum*)
                    Castor bean (*Ricinus communis*)
                    Sesame (*Sesamum indicum* or *S. orientale*)

FRUITS: Date palm (*Phoenix dactylifera*)
                    Dom palm (*Hyphaene thebaica*)
                    Egyptian plum (*Cordia myxa*)
                    Persea (*Mimusops schimperi*)
                    Peach (*Prunus persica*)
                    Watermelon (*Citrullus lunatus*)
                    Balanites (*Balanites aegyptiaca*)
                    Christ's thorn (*Ziziphus spina-Christi*)
                    Carob (*Ceratonia siliqua*)
                    Sycamore fig (*Ficus sycomorus*)

SEASONINGS: Coriander (*Coriandrum sativum*)

NUTS: Pine nut (*Pinus* cf. *pinea*)

FODDER: cf. Bittervetch (*Vicia ervilia*)

WILD PLANTS: Sedge (*Cyperus* sp.)
                    Acacia (*Acacia nilotica*)

WEEDS: Ryegrass (*Lolium temulentum*)
                    Canary grass (*Phalaris paradoxa*)
                    Medick (*Medicago hispida*)
                    Yellow vetchling (*Lathyrus aphaca*)
                    Vetch (*Vicia lutea*)
                    cf. Gromwell (*Buglossoides* sp.)

Tables 5.1 and 5.2, summarizing the plant remains, indicate the quantities of each and their provenience. In Table 5.2, the materials are listed by level for comparisons. In the section below, each of the types is described in detail.

Wheat

Today wheat (*Triticum* spp.) is one of the world's major foods, a position it has held for many millennia. Emmer wheat (*Triticum dicoccum* Schübel) (Plate 5.1a) was among the first plants domesticated in Southwest Asia and subsequently became the major cereal of the ancient Mediterranean world along with barley (Helback 1970:207). It has been cultivated in Egypt since at least 5000-4500 B.C., as evidenced by finds of emmer grains at the early Neolithic sites of Kom W in the Fayyum (Caton-Thompson and Gardner 1934:46-49) and Merimde in the Delta (Täckholm et al. 1941:242). Throughout the Pharaonic period emmer wheat and barley were staples. Emmer grains were used primarily for bread and occasionally for brewing (Täckholm et al. 1941:247-249), while the straw, presently called *tibn* in Arabic, was almost certainly an important summer fodder, as it is now (Dudgeon and Balland 1916:3). Wheat and barley crops were taxed annually and supplied much of the state's revenue. The grains, in turn, were one of the major forms of payment and wages used by the state and the temple (Erman 1894:123-125, Kemp 1972:659). As the staff of life, wheat, along with barley, figured constantly in offerings, ritual, and art.

Throughout the Persian period, emmer, a hulled wheat, continued as the staple, but after Alexander's conquest it was supplanted by a free-threshing wheat. Egypt's new conquerors reorganized, intensified, and improved agriculture, focusing much of their attention on wheat, in order to increase their revenues. Wheat was particularly lucrative because of the great demand for it in the markets of the Mediterranean world, especially in Greece (Rostovtsev 1941:359-60, 365-66). However, the Egyptian staple, emmer wheat, called *olyra* in Greek, was no longer popular, having been replaced by a free-threshing or naked wheat. The Ptolemies, accordingly, ordered vast plantings of naked wheat, experimenting with several varieties (Rostovtsev 1941:366). The new crop quickly took hold, and within 150 years the shift from emmer to free-threshing wheat was almost complete (Crawford 1979:140). Unlike emmer, which is tightly held by the glumes and hull, the grains of naked wheat separate easily during threshing. The most important of these new wheats appears to have been durum or hard wheat (*Triticum durum* Desf.) (Crawford 1979:140), presently cultivated for pasta products. Another naked wheat, bread wheat (*T. aestivum* L.) may have also been grown in Graeco-Roman Egypt (Täckholm et al. 1941:254-255). Greek papyri from the Fayyum offer evidence of the importance of the new wheat. They report that naked wheat occupied between 50-75% of the sown land while emmer represented less than 2% of the land (Crawford 1971:114-115). However, the temple lands showed a higher proportion of emmer. For example, a report for the sacred land near Aphroditopolis in the Fayyum records emmer occupying 27% the sown land and naked wheat 49% (Crawford 1971:115).

The el-Hibeh wheat remains include both the older emmer and the new naked wheat. Emmer, the more abundant of the two, is well represented by large quantities of spikelet remains, some of which are probably threshing debris. During threshing the spike separates into individual spikelets consisting of the internode or spike stem fragment, with connected glumes tightly wrapped around the grains. After vigorous pounding, the spikelets release the grains (Helbaek 1970:209) leaving behind the glumes and internode as a single unit resembling a tiny fork.

The el-Hibeh emmer fork specimens include the flattened, stem-like internode, approximately 2 to almost 3 mm in length. Narrow at the base, it widens at the apex where the "prongs," the hard, woody glumes, flare out. On the ventral surface, the side facing the central axis, two abscission scars can be seen, one at each end, marking the places where the adjoining spikelets were once attached. Many of the specimens are well-preserved with a glossy, reddish yellow to brown surface. The poorer specimens, not as well-preserved, consist of internode or glume fragments.

In one sample (provenience number: TS2 LEVEL 8 Lot 1A 316B), the spikelets apparently had not been threshed at the time they were deposited. Each spikelet is more or less complete, although most of the grains' endosperm has decomposed. Two spikelets are attached to each other, suggesting that they and the others may have been deposited as complete spikes that broke apart over time or during the jostling process of excavation.

The free-threshing wheat is represented by rachis or spike fragments. Unlike emmer wheat, the tough rachis of this form holds together during threshing as the grains and glumes fall away. The specimens consist of internodes positioned alternately on opposite sides of the central axis. Approximately 1.5 mm wide at the center and 3 to 4 mm long, the internodes are flattened, but at both ends they curve in toward the central axis. The narrowest point is at the base, while the top flares slightly. Here the broken stubs of the glumes indicate where the grains were once attached. Most of the specimens are hard and woody with a glossy reddish brown surface and hairs along the margins. The specimens may represent either durum or bread wheat, since the rachis is not sufficiently diagnostic to distinguish the two species (van Zeist 1976:36-37). However, durum is the more reasonable choice since it predominated during Ptolemaic times. In addition, durum is the only naked wheat reported from Ptolemaic sites in the adjacent Fayyum.

It is not surprising that wheat grains were scarce at el-Hibeh. They would not be expected to appear in household trash and the few that might have been accidently discarded would probably not preserve well. Indeed, little remains of the few grains that were found. Most consist of no more than the durable outer coating, the endosperm having decomposed. The only two complete wheat grains found are ellipsoid, with rounded ends and convex flanks. The ventral surface is somewhat flattened while the dorsal is rounded and has a wide longitudinal ridge. The cross-section is rounded triangular with the widest part of the grain in the center. The ventral furrow is V-shaped and uniform in width. Both specimens have a rectangular patch of hair on the apex. One grain is reddish-brown while the other is a golden yellow. The dimensions, 6.1 x 2.9 x 2.7 mm and 4.9 x 2.2 x 1.8 mm, are small for wheat and suggest that these may have been the undersized grains found in the terminal position of the spike. Because of their size they may have been winnowed away with the chaff. Their characteristics resemble hard wheat more than emmer wheat, but with such a small sample they can only be called wheat with certainty.

Barley

Barley (*Hordeum vulgare* L.) (Plate 5.1a) was one of the first plants domesticated in Southwest Asia and for several millennia has been one of the world's major crops. Today it is grown throughout the world primarily for animal feed and for malt used in brewing and manufacturing various food products. In some areas barley also serves as human food in the form of parched grains, porridge, flour for flat breads, and pearled grains for soup (Wiebe 1979:1). Barley has been known in Egypt since at least 5000-4000 B.C.; as noted above, barley was found with emmer wheat at early Neolithic sites in the Fayyum (Caton-Thompson and Gardner 1934:46-49) and at Merimde (Täckholm et al. 1941:288). Throughout Pharaonic times hulled barley was one of the major crops supplying grains for brewing beer, feeding livestock, and making bread (Darby et al. 1977:484). Barley remained an important crop during Graeco-Roman times but was far surpassed by wheat in total production. For example, Greek papyri from the Ptolemaic Fayyum indicate that barley occupied between 2-16% of the cultivated crown land and even less of the private land (Crawford 1971:113). Today barley is still a major crop in Egypt, serving primarily as fodder (Jones 1934:1). Modern Egyptians also use barley to make *subia*, a nonalcoholic beverage, and *bouza*, an alcoholic drink, as well as to prepare bread, either alone or with other cereals (Täckholm et al. 1941:284).

The barley from el-Hibeh includes both kernels and rachis segments, all of the six-rowed, hulled variety. The rachis fragments consist of single internodes, the individual units of the spike, and segments of several internodes still attached to each other. Most of the specimens are well-preserved with a glossy surface and a reddish-brown color. The individual internodes are flattened stems approximately 1.4 mm wide, rounded at the base where they formerly attached to the adjacent internode and flaring at the apex to accommodate three grains, a diagnostic feature of six-rowed barley. The best preserved specimens retain their paper-thin, narrow glumes at the apex and the long hairs on the rachis edge. The specimens are fairly uniform in length ranging from 2.9 to 4.4 mm from the base to the apex.

The remains of the kernels consist of the caryoposis, or grain, and lemma and palea, or hulls, which adhere tightly to the grains in the hulled form. Few specimens are well-preserved; in most cases the grain has partially decomposed. However, the stiff hulls retain the shape of the kernel, which is spindle-like with a blunt embryo end and a truncated apex where the awn, a long, needle-like structure, has broken off. Both dorsal and ventral surfaces are rounded in the middle, while the flanks also flare at the center. As a result the widest part of the grain is in the center, where the cross-section is elliptical. Several of the grains are asymmetrical, twisting slightly at the embryo end, another characteristic of six-rowed barley. In the three-grained spikelet of the six-rowed form the two grains on the sides, or lateral positions, grow in a curved fashion while the grain in the center is straight. The lengths of the kernels vary from 9.1 to 11.1 mm, while the width is more constant, ranging from 2.7 to 3.5 mm. In addition to the kernels, a large number of lemma and palea fragments were recovered.

Olive

The olive tree (*Olea europaea* L.) (Plate 5.1b), a native of the eastern Mediterranean region, has been cultivated here since prehistoric times for its fruit, an oily drupe (Renfrew 1973:134). The fleshy mesocarp of the fruit is eaten fresh (Renfrew 1973:134) or pickled either green or ripe (Brouk 1975:117). The ripe olive is also pressed for its oil, which represents up to 50% of the weight (Meyer 1980:416) and is a major cooking and table oil in the Mediterranean region.

Adapted to cool winters and warm dry summers, the olive tree is cultivated only in northern Egypt today—the Fayyum, the western Mediterranean coast (Täckholm 1961:28), and Siwa Oasis (Darby et al. 1977:718). Records of the olive in ancient Egypt go back to the Pyramid texts of the 5th and 6th Dynasties, and Reisner suggests that the oil was imported from Palestine as early as the 6th Dynasty (Täckholm 1961:28). But there are no archaeological traces of olives during the Pharaonic period until the 18th Dynasty, when Egyptians began the practice of placing a small crown of olive leaves around the forehead of the mummy (Täckholm 1961:29). Abundant evidence does not appear until the Graeco-Roman period (Täckholm 1961:29; Darby et al. 1977:720). Under the Ptolemies, olive trees were planted extensively, especially in the Fayyum, primarily to provide the Greek population of Egypt with olive oil (Rostovtsev 1941:355-356). Unlike other oil-producing plants, olives were not regulated by the strict oil monopoly of the crown (outlined in the *Revenue Laws of Ptolemy Philadelphus*), but they probably were controlled in some way by the state (Rostovtsev 1941:356).

The olive stones from el-Hibeh, all desiccated and well-preserved, vary in size and shape, ranging from 11.9 to 22.1 mm in length and 6.1 to 11.0 mm in diameter. The stones, more or less symmetrical, are spindle-shaped with pointed ends and a round cross-section. The surface, a light, dull brown, is covered with irregular longitudinal grooves.

Flax

Probably domesticated in Southwest Asia (van Zeist 1976:32), flax (*Linum usitatissimum* L.) (Plate 5.1b) is now cultivated in Europe, North America, and Asia for its fibers and seeds. The former, extracted from the stems, are woven into linen, while the seeds are used mainly as a source of linseed oil with the residue serving as animal fodder (Hedrick 1919:337). However, the seeds are edible, if treated properly, and have been eaten as a cereal. Pliny reported that the Romans used roasted flax seed with barley and coriander in a porridge, while Thucydides states that the Greeks also ate the seeds (Hedrick 1919:332).

Flax has been known in Egypt since Neolithic times; fragments of linen fabric and flax seeds were found at Neolithic sites in the Fayyum (Caton-Thompson and Gardner 1934:49). Throughout Pharaonic times flax was the major source of fabric for the living as well as the dead and continued to be important during the Graeco-Roman Period. Under the Ptolemies the production of linseed oil, used for lighting, was tightly controlled by a state monopoly, while linen weaving was also government regulated (Rostovtsev 1941:302,306).

The el-Hibeh flax specimens consist of small fragments of the fruit capsule. Desiccated and well-preserved, the most complete specimens are from a globular capsule with a smooth brown exterior marked with a series of irregularly spaced longitudinal lines and ridges. The interior shows traces of the septa delineating each of the separate chambers which once held a seed. These fragments could represent discards from any number of activities. They may have come from seed stock used for planting or they might have been discarded after the seeds were threshed for the oil factory or for home consumption. The fragments might also have come from ripe plants harvested for the tough fibers that are used for ropes and mats (Lucas and Harris 1962:143).

Castor Oil Plants

A familiar tree of the Egyptian countryside, the castor oil plant (*Ricinus communis* L.

called *kheraway* in Arabic) is cultivated for its oil-rich seeds (Plate 5.1b). Ricinoleic acid, its major oil constituent, is used today in a wide variety of industrial processes, in the pharmaceutical industry, and in lubricants (Colonial Plant and Animal Products 1955:165). The villagers in Upper Egypt also use the plant in a variety of ways. The stems pull *shadoofs*, the leaves serve for drying wounds, and the oil is a purgative, an unguent for women's skin and scalps, and a remedy for animal scab disease (Gadalla 1924-25:63). In addition the oil has been used for cooking in the Sudan (Ruffer 1919:83) and China (Hedrick 1919:503), although many people consider the flavor unpleasant.

The castor oil plant has been known in Egypt at least since Predynastic times, as indicated by desiccated bean specimens found in a grave at Badari (Brunton and Caton-Thompson 1928:38). Charred specimens were also found at the Predynastic site of Ma'adi (Keimer 1936:70-71). During Pharaonic times the castor bean was one of the four major sources of oil (Ruffer 1919:79). It served primarily for lighting (Montet 1981:90), but the poor also used it as an unguent in lieu of more expensive oils. Ruffer (1919:83) suggests that they may have cooked with it as well. The castor oil plant also offered a variety of medicinal properties to the ancient Egyptians. The root, crushed in water, was applied to the head of a sick man to make him well immediately. The seeds (chewed with beer) were taken for diarrhea. Ground and mixed with oil, the seeds were rubbed on the head in hopes of restoring hair (Darby et al. 1977:788).

The castor beans from el-Hibeh, desiccated and well-preserved, are nearly all complete ellipsoid-shaped seeds. Rather uniform in size, they range from 9.9 to 11.6 mm in length, 6.5 to 7.9 mm in width, and 4.9 to 5.4 mm in thickness. The testa, still shiny but brittle, is dull beige mottled with brown splotches.

Sesame

A native of tropical East Africa, sesame (*Sesamum indicum* L. or *S. orientale*) (Plate 5.1b) is an annual herb cultivated today in India, Africa, Central America, Mexico, and the U.S. for its oil-rich seeds (Brouk 1975:327). Small and pear-shaped, the seeds occur in capsules that burst open when ripe (Brouk 1975:327). Whole, the seeds are used in confections in the Middle East, China, and India. Pounded, the seeds make a flavorful paste, called *taheena* in Arabic, which is popular as a dip, a sauce, and a cooking ingredient in the Middle East. The seeds may also be pressed for their oil, which represents 45-55% of the seed and is popular in cooking (Brouk 1975:241).

Archaeological evidence of sesame is scarce for ancient Egypt, but Darby and his associates (1977:786) suggest that it probably was an important source of oil since olives could not have covered all of Egypt's needs for cooking and lamp oil. Ruffer (1919:790) believes it was the favorite cooking oil, imported from Syria. There is no evidence of the plant on monuments but by the 3rd century B.C. there is good documentary evidence that it was cultivated in Egypt. Theophrastus reported on it, and several economic papyri discussed sesame paste and oil (Darby et al. 1977:786).

The sesame specimen from el-Hibeh is the lower end of the seed capsule with a fragment of the pedicel still attached. A dull beige-brown, the capsule is four-chambered, approximately 7 mm across. About 17 mm long, the fragment represents the lower 1/3 or 1/4 of a complete capsule.

Date

One of the most familiar trees of the Egyptian landscape, the date palm (*Phoenix dactylifera* L.) (Plate 5.2) has a tall, unbranched trunk surmounted by a crown of leaves. It is one of Egypt's most valuable trees, with virtually every part serving humans in some way. The fruit, a berry, is eaten fresh or dried and can be used in distilling a strong liquor. Fruits that are green or of poor quality serve as fodder. The vegetative parts of the tree are used as a construction material and in making bags, ropes, mats, and baskets (El-Hadidi and Boulos 1979:83).

The date palm was equally well appreciated in ancient Egypt. The tree and fruits were frequently illustrated in reliefs and frescoes, while various parts of the palm served as motifs in architecture, jewelry, amulets, and furniture (Darby et al. 1977:729). Archaeological evidence of date fruits and date cakes are abundant from the Middle Kingdom on (Täckholm 1961:8). In addition, documentary sources dating from the New Kingdom indicate that date juice was used to make wine and to flavor beer, while date fruits and seeds served a wide variety of medicinal functions (Darby et al. 1977:729-730). Täckholm (1961:8) suggests that prior to the Middle Kingdom only the vegetative parts of the plant were used because Egyptians did not yet know how to carry out artificial pollination in the dioecious palm. However, date fruits certainly were available in Egypt before this time but probably became far more abundant after artificial pollination was introduced. In natural groves where male and female plants are equally common, wind pollination is adequate to fertilize the fruits, according to Brown and Boghot (1938:43). The advantage of artificial pollination is that it assures uniform fertilization for all female trees even where male trees might be scarce.

Date seeds were the most abundant plant type in this collection from el-Hibeh, accounting for over 1100 specimens, or some 62% of the materials recovered. The hard seeds, nearly all desiccated, are cylindrical with a round cross-section and a deep longitudinal furrow on one side. Some of the seeds retain papery traces of the reddish fleshy fruit. The specimens range widely in size and shape from short, squat bulky seeds to long, thin ones with pointed ends. The dimensions vary from 14.4 to 34.6 mm in length and 6.1 to 10.0 mm in diameter. The wide variation in size and shape could indicate that a number of different varieties were imported from elsewhere, since varieties today are characteristic of particular regions (Brown and Boghot 1939:70). Alternatively the range could reflect natural variation resulting from changes in growing conditions or other factors. Brown and Boghot (1938:46) note that date fruits can vary widely in size even on a single branch.

Dom Palm

Part of the wild flora of Upper Egypt, the dom palm (*Hyphaene thebaica* [L.] Mart.) (Plate 5.2) is recognized by its forked trunk and fan-shaped leaves. The glossy brown globular fruits have a fibrous, sugary mesocarp said to taste like ginger (Täckholm 1961:9). After soaking, it can be eaten raw or prepared as a syrup (Darby et al. 1977:730). The hard stone inside the fruit, a vegetable ivory, is used in making buttons, rings, beads, and other objects (Täckholm 1961:9).

The hard, nearly indestructable fruits are well-represented in the archaeological record and indicate that dom palm fruits have been used in Egypt at least since the Predynastic

(Täckholm and Drar 1950:282). Ancient Egyptians also used the wood and stone for making small objects and as a construction material, while the fibers were used in mats (Darby et al. 1977:732).

The el-Hibeh specimens include fragments and three complete fruits. The latter are irregularly globoid with a longitudinal keel or ridge along one side and range from 45.7 to 52.0 mm in length and 39.7 to 44.0 mm in diameter. All of the fruits have been stripped of the mesocarp, but none appears to have been cut in order to extract the vegetable ivory. These are presumably the discards from dom fruits eaten in the village, which may have been imported from Upper Egypt or may have come from the few rare dom palms seen in this part of the country.

Egyptian Palm

Called *mokheit* in Arabic, the Egyptian plum (*Cordia myxa* L.) (Plate 5.3a) is cultivated today along Egypt's Mediterranean coast and in the oases for its fruit (Täckholm 1961:29). A small orange drupe, the fruit is sweet and somewhat astringent (Täckholm 1961:29). Now used primarily for making bird-lime, it was enjoyed as a fruit as well as a wine in ancient Egypt (Täckholm 1961:29, Darby et al. 1977:707). Fruit stones of Egyptian plum have been recovered from archaeological sites of all periods in Egypt beginning with the 3rd Dynasty (Täckholm 1961:29).

Egyptian plum is represented at el-Hibeh by fifteen desiccated fruit stones, most of which are complete specimens. A dull pale brown, the stones are ellipsoid with a pointed apex and blunt base. Slightly flattened the stones have two sharp ridges running from base to apex along the widest part of the stone where the two hemispheres join. Small, irregular ridges cover most of the remaining surface. The specimens are fairly uniform ranging from 9.4 to 12.5 mm in length, 7.9 to 10.5 mm in width, and 5.0 to 7.9 mm in thickness.

Persea

A native of Arabia and tropical Africa, *Mimusops schimperi* Hochst. the *persea* of Graeco-Roman times (Plate 5.3a) was cultivated extensively in the gardens of ancient Egypt, although it is now nearly extinct (Lauer et al. 1950:129). Considered sacred to both Isis and Osiris, the tree was often depicted with the pharaoh in reliefs and paintings (Darby et al. 1977:740). The twigs and leaves served in funeral garlands and formal bouquets, while the wood was used for statues, tables, beds, and other objects (Täckholm 1961:27). The fruit, edible and abundant, was much esteemed and often used in tomb offerings, the earliest known example dating from the 3rd Dynasty (Lauer et al. 1950:130). Theophrastus described the fruit as:

> . . . large as a pear, but in shape it is oblong, almond-shaped, and its colour is grass green. It has inside a stone like the plum, but much smaller and softer; the flesh is sweet and luscious and easily digested; for it does not hurt if one eats it in quantity. (Theophrastus 4,2,5 quoted in Darby et al. 1977:736).

The el-Hibeh persea seeds, desiccated and well-preserved, vary in shape and size. They are roughly elliptical in outline, somewhat flattened with a ridge encircling the seed along this edge. The cross-section varies from an irregular ellipse to an asymmetrical diamond or a triangle with rounded edges. In most specimens the testa is a shiny reddish brown. Near one end of the seed the hilum appears as a notch in the testa. The dimensions of the seeds range from 17.1 to 25.4 mm in length, 9.1 to 14.4 mm in width and 5.9 to 9.1 mm in thickness.

Peach

The peach tree (*Prunus persica* Stokes.) (Plate 5.2), a native of China, was apparently brought to the Eastern Mediterranean several centuries before the birth of Christ, probably by way of Persia (Hedrick 1919:463, Darby et al. 1977:735). The fruit, a drupe, may have been introduced into Egypt during the late Dynastic Period (Darby et al. 1977:735), but the tree was probably not systematically cultivated in Egypt until the Greek period. The Ptolemies, in their efforts to extend viticulture, made extensive plantings of fruit trees, including peaches, in new orchards and plantations, especially in the Fayyum (Crawford 1979:140).

Most archaeological evidence of peaches comes from Roman and Coptic sites (Täckholm 1961:15), but peach stones have been found at the Graeco-Roman town of Karanis (Crawford 1979:138).

Peach stones were abundant and well-preserved at el-Hibeh. Varying in size and shape, the light brown stones are more or less pyriform in outline, with a rounded base and pointed apex. The juncture of the two cotyledons is marked in most specimens by a sharp ridge. In cross-section they are more or less elliptical and symmetrical, but several specimens display a wide gap along one side where the cotyledons meet. All specimens are covered with a series of deep irregular grooves and pits (most of which are oriented longitudinally), characteristic of peach stones. The dimensions range from 21.2 to 31.3 mm in length, 16.1 to 20.8 mm in width and 13.3 to 18.6 mm in thickness.

Watermelon

A native of Africa, the watermelon or sweet melon (*Citrullus lunatus* formerly *Citrullus vulgaris*) (Plate 5.3a) is cultivated throughout warm regions of the world (Brouk 1975:202). Its sweet, juicy flesh is one of the most popular summer fruits in Egypt. A small inedible melon, *Citrullus vulgaris* Schrad var *colocynthoides*, is also cultivated in Egypt and imported from the Sudan. Its seeds, similar to those of the sweet melon, are roasted and sold as a snack called *libb* in Arabic (Täckholm 1961:31). Both varieties have been known in Egypt since Pharaonic times. The oldest known examples of *libb* seeds come from a 5th Dynasty site (Täckholm 1961:31), while leaves and seeds of the sweet melon have been recovered from New Kingdom tombs (Darby et al. 1977:718, Ruffer 1919:63).

During Graeco-Roman times a third melon was cultivated for its seeds, which contained about 15% oil (Ruffer 1919:83). Referred to as *colocynthos* in the Greek texts (Rostovtsev 1941:302), the identification is uncertain, but Ruffer (1919:83) suspects that it was *Citrullus colocynthus*, a small wild melon growing on the deserts, called *handal* in Arabic. Another possibility is that the plant was the same as the *libb* melon already under cultivation.

The el-Hibeh specimens, which may represent all of these types, are flattened, ovate seeds, rounded at one end, narrowing at the other. The margins are smooth and rounded except at the narrow end of the specimen where a shallow incision, 2 to 3 mm long, runs along the edge of the seed to the tip on both dorsal and ventral sides. The surface of the testa on all but one specimen has eroded away to a dull beige to pale brown. The exception has a well-preserved testa, light brown mottled with black, which is characteristic of the sweet melon. The others may be badly eroded specimens of the same or they may be the bitter type melon. The dull brown specimens, ranging from 10.0 to 11.5 mm in length and 5.8 to 6.7 mm in width, fall within the size range of modern *libb* seeds, purchased in Egyptian markets, which rarely exceed 11 to 12 mm in length. The dark brown seed, 12.6 x 6.7 mm, is within the size range of modern sweet watermelon seeds which are over 12 or 13 mm in length. The thickness of all the seeds ranges from 1.7 to 2.6 mm.

Balanites

Rare in Egypt today, *Balanites* (*Balanites aegyptiaca* Del.) (Plate 5.2) was an important and apparently common plant of ancient Egypt. A thorny shrub or tree, now called *heglig* in Arabic, it bears fleshy edible drupes that were enjoyed as a fruit (Täckholm 1974:313), while the inner "almond" of the stone was the source of balanos oil used in making precious unguents (Lauer et al. 1950:132, Täckholm 1961:23). Archaeological *Balanites* stones, common in pharaonic tombs, often have perforations that were apparently used to extract the oil.

The two el-Hibeh *Balanites* fruit stones are well-preserved, complete specimens. Ellipsoid with a rounded cross-section, they are pointed at both ends, narrowing more at one end than the other. Five shallow furrows run the length of the stones, which are about 29 and 35 mm long with maximum diameters of 13 and 12 mm respectively. A dull, dark beige, both stones are relatively smooth, but fine splinter fragments pull away from the specimens at both ends. Unlike many archaeological finds of *Balanites*, these stones have not been pierced.

Christ's Thorn

Sidder in Arabic, the Christ's thorn tree (*Ziziphus spina-Christi* Willd.) (Plate 5.3a) grows wild in southeast Egypt and is also cultivated throughout the country for its wood, edible fruits, and shade (El-Hadidi and Boulos 1979:124). The fruit, called *nabakh* in Arabic, is said to taste like an apple. It is rarely found in the markets but is popular in the countryside (Täckholm 1961:25). The fruit was popular in ancient Egypt as well and is documented in the archaeological record beginning with the Predynastic (Täckholm 1961: 25). The Ebers Papyrus records that the Christ's thorn fruit and leaves were used widely in medicine (Darby et al. 1977:703).

The one el-Hibeh *Ziziphus* specimen is a desiccated complete globoid fruit stone, 8.5 mm in diameter. A dull, light brown color, the stone is covered with a pattern of irregular ridges.

Carob

The carob tree (*Ceratonia siliqua* L.), (Plate 5.3a) a member of the legume family, is a native of the eastern Mediterranean region, where it is now widely cultivated for its seeds and fruit (Duke 1981:50, Brouk 1975:164). The latter, an indehiscent leathery brown pod, is extremely rich in sugar (Brouk 1975:164) and is used in foods, juices, and flour (Duke 1981:50). It was very popular in Europe until the beginning of the 20th century (Brouk 1975:164). The brown seeds of the carob are a coffee substitute when roasted and a source of gum used in many food products (Duke 1981:50).

In ancient Egypt the carob tree was cultivated for both the fruit and the wood. A variety of furniture and utensils, such as chairs, chests, tables, and chariots (Ruffer 1919:66), were made from the hard, heavy carob wood, which is still used today for furniture and wheels (Duke 1981:50). The pods served a variety of medicinal functions such as enemas and dressings (Darby et al. 1977:699), and the juice from the fruit was used in a mouth rinse (Darby et al. 1977:441). The pods were probably eaten as well, although Coit (1951) claims that they were used mainly as fodder in ancient times and were rarely eaten by humans because of the high fiber content. He believes that the carob did not become popular for humans until superior modern varieties were developed. However, it seems unlikely that carob pods would be found in tomb offerings with other foods if they had not been eaten. The oldest example of such an offering comes from the 12th Dynasty tomb at Kahun (Täckholm 1961:22).

Carob is represented at el-Hibeh by several seeds but no pod specimens. The seeds, all a dull black, are flattened, elliptical to rounded in outline, with a notch in the testa for the hilum. The ventral and dorsal surfaces of the seeds are slightly rounded, showing an elliptical cross-section. The dimensions range from 8.1 to 9.3 mm in length, 5.9 to 6.9 mm in width, and 3.1 to 4.6 mm in thickness.

Sycamore Fig

A popular tree in Egypt today, the sycamore fig (*Ficus sycomorus* L.) (Plate 5.2), called *gimmeiz* in Arabic, is valued for its shade and fruit. The latter, a syconium rather than a true botanical fruit, is a hollow, fleshy receptacle that becomes sweet and juicy as it ripens, like the better known commercial fig (El-Hadidi and Boulos 1979:64). Before it ripens, the fruit is usually incised, allowing the interior to dry out. This practice, common in Egypt today, discourages the wasps that fertilize the flowers from laying eggs inside.

The sycamore fig is well-documented in the archaeological and textual record from Pharaonic times. The earliest fig specimens come from Predynastic graves at Mostagadda and the 1st Dynasty tombs at Abydos (Lauer et al. 1950:131). The sycamore fig was often depicted in paintings and reliefs and noted in religious texts such as the Book of the Dead and the Pyramid texts. It was considered sacred to Isis, Nephthys, Nut, and Hathor (Ruffer 1919:58). In addition, the fruit was valued for its medicinal properties. It was prescribed for the "blood-eater" affliction, which may have been scurvy, and was an ingredient in a variety of medicinal mixtures. Its leaves were applied to hippopotamus bites and its latex was used to darken scars (Darby et al. 1977:746). The wood was also a valuable material. Light and durable, it was used for sarcophagi and agricultural tools (El-Hadidi and Boulos 1979:64).

The el-Hibeh specimen is a single desiccated fruit, globoid, flattened at one end and pointed at the other where the pedicel is still attached. About 12 mm long and 14.5 mm in diameter, the fruit is a dull light brown. The surface is smooth except for fine longitudinal lines running from the pedicel to the base.

Coriander

An annual herb, native to the Mediterranean region, coriander (*Coriandrum sativum* L.) (Plate 5.3b) is cultivated as a seasoning. The fruit, a cremocarp, is used whole or ground after drying (Brouk 1975:297), while the young leaves may be put in soups and salads (Hedrick 1919:191). One of the most popular seasonings in Egyptian cuisine today, coriander is cultivated in the Nile Valley, but also grows wild in Egypt (Brouk 1975:297). The plant has probably been known in Egypt since Pharaonic times although the archaeological evidence is sparse. The earliest examples may be coriander seeds found in Tut-Ankh-Amun's 18th Dynasty tomb (Darby et al. 1977:798).

The el-Hibeh specimens consist of desiccated fragments of the fruit wall and can be identified on the basis of the globoid shape with points at both poles, as well as the surface features. The latter consist of a series of alternating wavy and straight longitudinal ridges. The fruits are approximately 4 to 5 mm in diameter.

Pine

The stone pine (*Pinus pinea* L.) (Plate 5.3b), found along the northern coast of the Mediterranean from Portugal to Syria (Meyer 1980:419), has provided timber and nuts to the Mediterranean world since ancient times. The delicious nuts, considered a delicacy by the ancient Romans (Meyer 1980:421), are still popular in Middle Eastern and southern European cuisine (Hedrick 1919:438). In ancient times the wood of the stone pine was considered one of the best for resisting rot and wood worms (Meyer 1980:421).

Pine cones, laden with nuts, were apparently imported into Egypt during Graeco-Roman times and possibly earlier. Specimens of nuts and cones have been found at several sites of this period, such as the Roman port of Quseir al-Qadim on the Red Sea coast (Wetterstrom 1982:372) and the Graeco-Roman Fayyum town of Karanis (Crawford 1979:138).

The el-Hibeh specimen is a single desiccated fragment of a pine cone scale. Representing the outer end of the scale, the fragment is flat, approximately 17 mm wide and 6 mm thick, with a raised irregular pentagon, characteristic of pine. A pale brown, the specimen closely matches stone pine cones from the site of Karanis and is most likely this type. However the scale fragment has not yet been compared with cones of the two pines that are cultivated in Egypt, Aleppo pine (*Pinus halepensis*) and chir pine (*P. longifolia*) (El-Hadidi and Boulos 1979:86,88).

Bitter Vetch

A native of the Mediterranean region, this annual legume (*Vicia ervilia* [L.] Willd.) (Plate 5.4b) is cultivated as a fodder crop throughout the Middle East (Duke 1981:275).

The beans are an excellent fodder (Duke 1981:276) and are sometimes used as a famine food (Zohary and Hopf 1973:893). The bitter principle, a cyanogenetic glycoside, which imparts an unpleasant taste to the beans, is toxic to pigs, horses, and poultry, but ruminants and humans are highly resistant to it (Meyer 1980:409). On the basis of large caches of the seeds found at Neolithic and Bronze Age sites, Helbaek (1970:227) suggests that during these periods bitter vetch may have been more popular as a human food than it is now. However, he cautions that not all bitter vetch finds come from cultivated plants, since weedy races are common throughout the Middle East and their seeds often contaminate grain crops (Zohary and Hopf 1973:89).

Bitter vetch has been known in Egypt since the Predynastic but was probably no more than a weed in the fields at this time (Wetterstrom, in press). During Graeco-Roman times the plant was apparently cultivated for fodder. Bitter vetch beans were common at the Fayyum town of Karanis (Wetterstrom, unpublished data) and the Roman port of Quseir al-Qadim (Wetterstrom 1982:367).

The el-Hibeh specimens are mere fragments of a legume testa that bear the features of bitter vetch but cannot be positively identified without more complete materials. The shriveled and curled specimens are a sandy to reddish brown color, mottled with dark brown. The contours of the fragments suggest a compressed spheroid seed somewhere between 3 and 5 mm in width. A number of the fragments exhibit a well-preserved ovate hilum, approximately 1.5 to 2.0 mm long. A slight ridge rises on all sides of the hilum and a prominent chalaza lies about 1.5 mm from the hilum. On the other side of the hilum the testa bends sharply forming an angle of about 90° to the plane on which the hilum lies. All of these features are characteristic of bitter vetch and would not be found in many other legumes from Egypt.

Sedge

The sedges (*Cyperus* L.) (Plate 5.4a), grass-like plants often growing in aquatic environments, include several species that have edible stems and underground parts—roots, tubers, or rhyzomes. Egyptians have relied on these as a source of food for many millennia. The most popular sedge in Egypt today, a plant called *habb el-'aziz* (*Cyperus esculentus*), has small sweet tubers that were an important food for ancient Egyptians (Täckholm 1961:8). Papyrus (*Cyperus papyrus*), the well-known source of paper, was also valued as a food among ancient Egyptians—both the stems and roots were eaten (Darby et al. 1977:645).

The el-Hibeh specimens include two desiccated complete rhyzomes or tubers, and fragments of a third. A dull, dark brown, the specimens are more or less cylindrical, slightly flattened, and have a rounded point at one end and a truncated, flattened surface at the other end. A series of concentric rings, each about 3 mm apart, cover the entire length of the specimens. Fiber tufts are scattered over the surface, marking the places where rootlets were once attached. Measuring approximately 22 and 26 mm in length with maximum diameters of about 14 and 17 mm, respectively, they are much larger than *habb el-'aziz* tubers, which are rounded and about 10 mm long (Täckholm 1961:8). They do not seem to be papyrus specimens either, since they do not resemble published illustrations of the latter (Ragab 1980:26-30). It appears that the specimens are another species of sedge, but identification will not be possible until modern reference materials can be consulted.

Acacia

A native of Africa, the acacia (*Acacia nilotica* [L.] Willd. ex Del.) (Plate 5.4a) is one of the most abundant and useful trees in Egypt. It provides welcome shade and a wide array of valuable products. Both the inner bark and pods are used in tanning leather, while the young bark is used as a fiber. The shoots and young pods provide forage for sheep, goats, and camels, and the seeds are excellent cattle feed. The wood, rich in resins, resists insects and water, making it particularly suitable for boats, construction, water pipes, well-planking, plows, and other implements. The wood also yields an excellent firewood and charcoal which is sold in the markets. In addition, the tree is tapped for gum arabic (Duke 1981:9-10). In Egypt acacia flowers and pods also provide medicine. At Kharga and Dakhla Oases the dried flowers are steeped as a tea for gall bladder trouble, and, ground, they are placed on embers to yield an incense for nasal congestion (Osborn 1968:173).

The ancient Egyptians, like their modern counterparts, made extensive use of acacia. It was one of the major sources of wood; the pods were used in tanning; and the yellow, ball-like flower heads were used in funeral garlands (Lauer et al. 1950:134). Archaeological finds of acacia wood and pods are abundant and date back to the Predynastic (Lauer et al. 1950:134). In addition, the Ebers Papyrus documents a variety of medicinal uses for acacia.

All of the specimens from el-Hibeh consist of desiccated pod segments each containing a single seed. The lentoid, dull brown pod segments are asymmetrical with a glabrous, slightly rough surface, and range from 10.7 to 12.8 mm in diameter. The sections of the pod that lie between the seeds protrude as narrow necks on either side of the disk, enclosing the seed, giving the acacia pod its "rosary-bead" appearance.

Ryegrass

Ryegrasses (*Lolium* spp.) (Plate 5.4b) are common weeds of cultivated fields in the Near East and Europe (Reed 1977:108-111). The most troublesome, poisonous ryegrass (*L. temulentum* L.) harbors under its seed coat a fungus that can be fatal to both humans and animals (Renfrew 1973:177). In modern Egypt it is found in wheat and barley fields of the Delta, the oases, and the Mediterranean region (Täckholm 1974:707). Ryegrass has been known as a crop impurity in this area since the Predynastic and was apparently a common weed. It was the most abundant contaminant in the grain offerings at the 3rd Dynasty Zoser complex and at the Middle Kingdom site of Abu Sir (Lauer et al. 1950:146). The specimens from the latter site were analyzed for the harmful fungus, *Endoconidium temulentum*, and found to be contaminated, indicating that the weed was potentially fatal even 4000 years ago (Lauer et al. 1950:146).

The el-Hibeh ryegrass specimens consist of grains still encased in their hulls. Ranging from 4.0 to 6.2 mm in length and 1.7 to 2.4 mm in width, they are cylindrical, narrowing at the ends, and have an elliptical cross-section. The lemma and palea or hulls have a shark-skin texture, characteristic of ryegrass, and are light brown. The best preserved specimens have an awn, a feature that distinguishes poisonous ryegrass from *L. perenne* (Renfrew 1973:176), which also grows in Egypt. The ventral surface has a long wide furrow outlined by a keel on the hulls. The most complete specimen still has an attached internode, approximately 1.5 mm long, which is connected at the base of the grain and runs along the ventral furrow toward the apex. Attached to the internode is the fragment of a grain and its glumes.

Like the ryegrass from Abu Sir and Zoser's tomb, these specimens appear to be the most abundant weed type. However, they may not have been the most frequent weed in the fields. The ryegrass grains, slightly smaller than wheat, were probably difficult to separate in threshing and winnowing and, as a result, they were often stored with the grains.

Canary Grass

A common weed of the Mediterranean region (Reed 1977:138), canary grass (*Phalaris paradoxa* L.) (Plate 5.4b) is found in Egypt in palm groves, fields, roadsides, and cultivated land (Täckholm 1974:741). It was apparently a common field weed in Pharaonic times; both seeds and spikelets of *P. paradoxa* have been found in threshing debris from 5th and 12th Dynasty sites (Täckholm et al. 1941:406). The earliest examples of desiccated canary grass specimens were found among the grain offerings in Zoser's 3rd Dynasty tomb (Lauer et al. 1950:144-145).

The three canary grass specimens from el-Hibeh are well-preserved complete caryopses still enveloped in their lemma and palea or hulls. Bright and shiny, the hulls look fresh except for the reddish color, which is much darker than modern material. Ovate and flattened, the specimens are blunt at the base, while the apex has a long, drawn-out point. The palea, which covers the dorsal side, has two distinctive nerves running the length of the fruit. The dimensions range from 3.4 to 4.0 mm in length, 1.4 to 1.5 mm in width, and 0.7 to 0.8 mm in thickness.

Medick

Medick (*Medicago hispida* Gaertn.) (Plate 5.46) is a common winter weed invading cultivated fields throughout Egypt (El-Hadidi and Kosinova 1971:362; Lauer et al. 1950:135). It has apparently been a nuisance in Egyptian fields since at least the 1st Dynasty; Emory and Saad found a carbonized medick pod among the cereal offerings in Hemaka's tomb at Saqqarah (Lauer et al. 1950:135). Later tombs dating throughout the Pharaonic period and into Graeco-Roman times have also produced medick pods as grain contaminants (Lauer et al. 1950:135-136).

The one medick specimen from el-Hibeh is a light brown desiccated pod spiraled three times around to form a disk 5.3 mm in diameter and 2.1 mm thick. Along the margins of the pod are spines approximately 0.5 mm long. The flat face of the pod is covered with a reticulate pattern.

Yellow Vetchling

A field weed, vetchling (*Lathyrus aphaca* L.) (Plate 5.4b) is common throughout Egypt as well as Europe. Although the plant is known primarily as a weed, its peas were sometimes eaten in Europe while they were young and tender. But Sturtevant cautions that "if eaten abundantly in the ripe state (they) are narcotic, producing severe headaches" (Hedrick 1919:327). In Egypt there is no evidence that the plant has ever served as food. It has been known as a field weed at least since the early Dynastic times; specimens of yellow vetchling seeds and pods were among the crop contaminants in the grain offerings of Zoser's tomb (Lauer et al. 1950:142).

The el-Hibeh specimen is a well-preserved, desiccated seed, compressed globose and measuring about 3.5 x 3.1 mm. The ovate hilum is about 1.2 mm long, and the testa is glossy black.

Vetch

Vicia lutea L. (Plate 5.4b), called *bakhr* or *bakhran* in Arabic, is a common weed of the Nile Valley, the oases, and the western Mediterranean coast (Täckholm 1974:275,876). Like the closely related *Vicia sativa*, *bakhr* was a common field weed during Pharaonic times. Its seeds and pods were abundant among the grain offerings in Zoser's tomb (Lauer et al. 1950:140). Still earlier examples of this vetch were recovered at the Predynastic site of el-Omari (Lauer et al. 1950:140).

The el-Hibeh vetch specimen is a single, desiccated, well-preserved globular seed measuring 5.2 x 5.1 x 4.6 mm. The testa is a glossy chocolate brown with an oblong hilum, 3.8 x 1.4 mm. Both the size of the seed and the hilum characteristics agree well with the diagnostic features Täckholm (Lauer et al. 1950:139) specifies for *V. lutea*. The el-Hibeh specimen, like other archaeological ones, was probably a grain contaminant. However, as a type of vetch, it could have served as fodder as well.

Gromwell

Growing in Europe, in western Asia, and occasionally in coastal Egypt, gromwell (*Buglossoides* sp. I. M. Johnston, formerly *Lithospermum*) (Plate 5.4b) is most abundant in irrigated and moist environments (Helbaek 1970:237). The plant has no apparent uses as fuel, fodder, or food, but it has been found at a large number of early Neolithic sites in the Near East along with other seemingly useless plants of the same family, the borages. Helbaek (1969:400) suggests that the plants were collected for dyes found in borage roots.

The el-Hibeh materials that have been tentatively identified as gromwell consist of one complete nutlet and several fragments, all of which have been burned. One fragment has turned into a hard, bone-like white material, a change which gromwell seeds frequently undergo during burning (Helbaek 1970:237). The others are black and glossy. The complete specimen is ovoid, pointed at one end and truncated at the base with a large, flat basal scar. A ridge runs along one side of the nutlet. The seed coat is extremely hard, bony, and thick and has a glossy, bumpy surface. The lengths range from 3.4 to 4.3 mm.

All of these features agree closely with published descriptions of gromwell. But the specimens have not yet been compared with reference material and may ultimately prove to be another member of the borage family, such as the closely-related bugloss (*Echium* sp.). Gromwell is found only along the coast today, as noted above, but its distribution may have changed over the last 2000 years. On the other hand, bugloss is now common in the Nile Valley. In any case, whichever type of borage the specimens prove to be, they were most likely weeds among the el-Hibeh grain crops.

Unknowns

A small number of specimens have not yet been identified for lack of appropriate modern reference materials. They include a legume pod, a small composite flower head, and several damaged seeds.

C. Discussion and Conclusions

With such a small biased sample, it is risky to draw any firm conclusions. However, the collection offers some glimpses into the foods and agricultural practices of late Pharaonic and Ptolemaic times and raises some interesting questions about the economy under the Ptolemies. The material is best understood as a sampling of household discards—the food waste, inedible parts, and accidental spills that were thrown out in the process of preparing and eating food. As such it offers useful information about household activities and processing techniques. But with its heavy bias for inedible waste products and hard substances, the sample cannot be trusted as a source of quantitative data about the relative importance of various foods. However, it offers some information about the significance of foods within particular classes.

Most of the major classes of Egyptian crops are represented including cereals, oil crops, and fruits. The cereals, although the major source of food in ancient Egypt, constitute a small fraction of the collection. The recovery techniques are partially responsible for their low frequency—nearly all the grain specimens were recovered as "hitchhikers" among the sediments in the sample bags. Undoubtedly a much larger collection will be recovered when the sediment samples are analyzed. Another factor accounting for the meager sample of grains is the location where they were recovered. Household middens would not be expected to produce large quantities of grain. Nearly all of a family's grain stock would have been consumed, leaving few traces behind. Only granaries or dumps where threshing debris was discarded should produce good samples of grains or chaff. Except for two samples, el-Hibeh's few odd fragments of rachis segments represent neither grain stores nor threshing debris. Most of the material looks very much like the bits of debris that one finds in "clean" grain from the markets today. The el-Hibeh samples therefore suggest that the grains were threshed elsewhere, possibly at the edge of the village, and stored as "clean" grain. This pattern may have become more common during Ptolemaic times. One sample from the earlier deposits consists of complete spikelets that appear to have been deposited as whole spikes. This suggests that some emmer may have been stored as whole heads, possibly because the seed stock was better protected in this form, or the heads may have been intended as animal feed. But with such a small sample of material it is difficult to draw any reliable conclusions. The other exceptional sample is a set of material from the Ptolemaic deposits which appears to be threshing debris, perhaps used as fodder for the animals in one of the neighboring households. The sample includes glumes, internode fragments, and weed seeds, as well as bitter vetch, a fodder plant, but contains little evidence of grains.

Like the grains, the oil plants are poorly represented, except for the olive. Differential preservation is partly responsible—the fragile sesame and flax capsules as well as castor beans are likely to crumble and decompose long before the hard olive stone. But other factors may be at work here as well. During Ptolemaic times, castor beans, flax, and sesame all fell under the strict control of a state monopoly, as noted earlier. Outlined in detail by the *Revenue Laws of Ptolemy Philadelphus* the monopoly operated in the following way:

> Every year the surface to be planted with oil-bearing crops was distributed by the central government among various nomes, by the local administration of each nome among its several villages, and by the village administration among the individual farmers. So many *arourae* had to be planted with one or other of the oil-producing plants, and outside the

allotted areas no one had the right to grow these specified plants. The responsibility for the exact execution of the 'sowing-plan' lay with the administration. Each farmer received from the government the necessary seed, which was paid back by him to the government. The crops were gathered under the watchful eyes of the administration and the contractors, the underwriters or guarantors responsible for the yield. The produce of the fields was measured, one-fourth of it was paid as a tax and the rest was taken over by the contractor, who paid to the farmers the price of the amount delivered by them. The rate of payment was fixed by a tariff published by the king. The contractor had then to deliver the amount collected to the government. It was transported to the government's barns and thence to the government's oil factories, located in towns and villages. No private mills were tolerated, with the sole exception of those belonging to the temples (Rostovtsev 1941:302-303).

If this system had been followed perfectly at el-Hibeh, few if any traces of oil plants should have been found, since the crops were carried directly from the fields to the central factories. However, these specimens might represent debris or spills from the seed stock distributed by the government. However, it seems unlikely that sesame capsules would appear among the seeds, since the latter are promptly dispersed from the capsule when it is ripe. Another possibility is that the el-Hibeh farmers simply withheld part of their crop from the conquerors. By late Ptolemaic times much of the system had broken down (Crawford 1971: 117) and the Ptolemies' contractors may not have been successful in collecting the oil crops.

Olives, as noted earlier, were not regulated in the same manner as the other oil crops, although they were important enough to merit some form of state control (Rostovtsev 1941:356). Most likely they would have been pressed in a central location under strict supervision. The el-Hibeh olive specimens, like the other oil plants, might represent a portion of the crop that farmers secretly withheld. Whatever the case, they were most probably used as a relish rather than a source of oil. Had they been pressed, the stones probably would have been badly damaged.

The most abundant plants at el-Hibeh were the fruits—primarily because most of these have a hard stone or seed which cannot be consumed and once discarded is likely to persist. Indeed, the most numerous specimens are the hardest and most durable, including date seeds and peach stones. In contrast, the less abundant persea seeds and Egyptian plum stones, although hard, can be shattered under foot. And the grape, a very popular fruit in Pharaonic Egypt, is not represented at all—probably because the seeds are small and do not preserve well.

Among the hard-seeded fruits, most types probably have about the same chance of being preserved, once discarded. Yet they are not all equally abundant. These differences presumably offer some insights into their relative importance. The date, which overwhelms both the Pharaonic and Ptolemaic samples, was obviously a very important fruit. This is not particularly surprising. The date palm is abundant, and bears fruit prolifically. In addition the fruits can be stored and eaten throughout the year. In contrast, *Balanites* and Christ's thorn, with hard, nearly indestructable fruit stones, were very scarce. This is not surprising either. The Christ's thorn bears a small crop of tiny fruits that are eaten when ripe and, to my knowledge, are never stored. *Balanites* stones were a source of precious *balanos* oil and as a result were probably not carelessly discarded. The dom palm, with its very hard woody fruit, is also poorly represented, as is to be expected. As noted earlier, the tree is rare in this region.

The one class of crop plants totally absent from the sample is pulses. There are no traces of lentils, chickpeas, or garden peas—all important crops during Pharaonic times. The fava bean, which became popular during Graeco-Roman times, is also absent. These plants presumably were as important at el-Hibeh as elsewhere in Egypt. The household trash middens are a poor place to recover such perishable items as pulses and could not be expected to produce a large sample. The pulses leave no waste product except the pod, which decomposes easily and may be used as fodder. The beans, consisting largely of endosperm, decompose readily if accidentally discarded, but most of them would have been consumed. The few legumes found in the samples, the field weeds, are poorly preserved, except for a few specimens, indicating conditions were not good for preserving these types of seeds.

Despite the small size of the sample, the el-Hibeh collection also offers some evidence of changes through time. As noted earlier, the materials document some of the new crops introduced by the Ptolemies, including naked wheat, olives, and peaches. Some of these specimens may prove to be particularly valuable in resolving the botanical identification of plants known only through documentary sources. The pine cone fragment and the olives also indicate Greek influence or possibly the presence of Greek settlers. On the other hand, the sample reflects a great deal of continuity and tradition in Egyptian agriculture. Most of the crops and all of the field weeds found here had been known in Egypt for millennia. And despite the Greek demand for naked wheat, emmer wheat is abundant in the el-Hibeh samples. Does this indicate that the conquerors were not as successful in carrying out their plans as they suggest in their papyri? Or was el-Hibeh a more traditional Egyptian village? Perhaps the temple brought unusual quantities of emmer into the village? Or alternatively, the villagers may have relied heavily on emmer, after turning over most of their naked wheat crops to the Ptolemaic administrators. Unfortunately, none of these questions can be answered at the present time.

The plant remains from el-Hibeh give us a tantalizing glimpse of the crops and farming practices of this community. They raise many fascinating questions about the crop economy and hold out the hope of answering them with the abundant and well-preserved plant resources yet to be analyzed in Cairo and still in the ground. In short, the site of el-Hibeh offers an opportunity to draw a detailed picture of ancient Egyptian agriculture of the 1st millennium B.C.

TABLE 5.1

Plant Remains from TS1 and TS2, el-Hibeh

PROVENIENCE	LATIN NAME	COMMON NAME	PLANT PART	NUMBER
TS1a, Lv 5	*Cordia myxa*	Egyptian plum	Fruit stone	7
	Olea europaea	Olive	Fruit stone	3 whole, 6 halves
	Phoenix dactylifera	Date	Seed	86 + fragments
	Prunus persica	Peach	Fruit Stone	15 + fragments
	*Triticum cf. *durum*	Naked wheat; cf. hard wheat	Internode	4 fragments
	Ziziphus spina-christi	Nabakh	Fruit Stone	1
TS1a, Lv 5 A	**Coriandrum sativum*	Coriander	Capsule	1 fragment
	*Hordeum vulgare	Barley	Internode	1
			Glume	1 fragment
	*Triticum cf. *durum*	Naked wheat; cf. hard wheat	Internode	1
			Glume	1 fragment
TS1a, Lv 5 NE Corner	*Ceratonia siliqua*	Carob	Seed	4
	Cordia myxa	Egyptian plum	Fruit stone	3 + fragments
	Coriandrum sativum	Coriander	Capsule	1 fragment
	Linum usitatissimum	Flax	Capsule	1 fragment
	Medicago hispida	Medick	Seed	1
	Mimusops schimperi	Persea	Seed	3
			Cotyledon	2
	Olea europaea	Olive	Fruit stone	8
	Phoenix dactylifera	Date	Seed	58 + fragments
	Pinus sp.	Pine	Cone bract	1
	Prunus persica	Peach	Fruit stone	7 + fragments
TS1a, Lv 5 Lot 1	*Ceratonia siliqua*	Carob	Seed	1
TS1a, Lv 5 #219	*Phoenix dactylifera*	Date	Seed	7
TS1a, Lv 6	*Olea europaea*	Olive	Fruit stone	3
	Phoenix dactylifera	Date	Seed	62
TS1a, Lv 6 NE Lot 3	*Olea europaea*	Olive	Fruit stone	2
	Phoenix dactylifera	Date	Seed	62
TS1a, Lv 7 Lot 4	*Phoenix dactylifera*	Date	Seed	15
	*Triticum cf. *durum*	Naked wheat; cf. hard wheat	Rachis segment	1
TS1a, Lv 10 Lot 7	*Balanites aegyptiaca*	Balanites	Fruit stone	1
	Cordia myxa	Egyptian plum	Fruit stone	1
	Olea europaea	Olive	Fruit stone	1
	Phoenix dactylifera	Date	Seed	35

*These plants were found among the sediments in the sample bags and were not collected systematically.

PROVENIENCE	LATIN NAME	COMMON NAME	PLANT PART	NUMBER
TS1a, Lv 11	*Mimusops schimperi*	Persea	Seed	1 fragment
Lot 8			Cotyledon	1 fragment
	Olea europaea	Olive	Fruit stone	3 + fragments
	Phoenix dactylifera	Date	Seed	31 + fragments
	Prunus persica	Peach	Fruit stone	5
	Hordeum vulgare	Barley	Hull	Fragments
TS1a, Lv 12	**Hordeum vulgare*	Barley	Hull	Fragments
Lot 8	*Hyphaene thebaica*	Dom	Mesocarp	1 fragment
	*Triticum cf. *durum*	Naked wheat; cf. hard wheat	Glume	Fragments
TS1b, Lv 1 A	*Mimusops schimperi*	Persea	Seed	1
	Olea europaea	Olive	Fruit stone	2 halves
	Phoenix dactylifera	Date	Seed	16 + fragments
TS1b, Lv 1 B	*Cordia myxa*	Egyptian plum	Fruit stone	1
	Olea europaea	Olive	Fruit stone	1
	Phoenix dactylifera	Date	Seed	15 + fragments
TS1b, Lv 3	*Phoenix dactylifera*	Date	Seed	19 + fragments
	Prunus persica	Peach	Fruit stone	2 + fragments
	*Triticum dicoccum	Emmer wheat	Internode	2
TS1b, Lv 4	**Hordeum vulgare*	Barley	Rachis segment	1
Lot 1 A	*Mimusops schimperi*	Persea	Seed	1 fragment
	*Triticum cf. *durum*	Naked wheat; cf. hard wheat	Rachis segment	12
			Spikelet	1
			Glume base	1
TS1b, Lv 4	*Mimusops schimperi*	Persea	Seed	1 + fragments
TS1b, Lv 5	*Balanites aegyptiaca*	Balanites	Fruit stone	1
Lot 3	*Mimusops schimperi*	Persea	Seed	Fragments
#290	*Phoenix dactylifera*	Date	Seed	2
	*Triticum dococcum	Emmer wheat	Spikelet	1
TS1b, Lv 6	**Lolium temulentum*	Darnel	Grain	1
Lot 1	*Triticum dicoccum*	Emmer wheat	Spikelet	1
			Glume	Fragments
	Vicia lutea	Vetch	Seed	1
TS1b, Lv 6	*Lolium temulentum*	Ryegrass	Spikelet	1
Lot 1				
TS1b, Lv 7	*Acacia nilotica*	Acacia	Seed w/pod	1
#333	**Citrullus lunatus*	Watermelon	Seed	1 + fragments
	Cyperus sp.	Sedge	Rhyzome	2
	Ficus sycomorus	Sycamore fig	Fruit	1
	Hordeum vulgare	Barley	Rachis segment	4
	Hyphaea thebaica	Dom	Mesocarp w/stone	1

PROVENIENCE	LATIN NAME	COMMON NAME	PLANT PART	NUMBER
TS1b, Lv 7	*Linum usitatissimum*	Flax	Capsule	Fragments
#333	*Mimusops schimperi*	Persea	Seed	1
(Continued)	*Phalaris paradoxa*	Canary grass	Grain	1
	Phoenix dactylifera	Date	Seed	1
	Ricinus communis	Castor bean	Seed	6 + fragments
	Sesamum indicum	Sesame	Capsule	1 **fragment**
	Triticum dicoccum	Emmer wheat	Spikelet	3
			Glume base	4
TS1b, Lv 7 B	**Acacia nilotica*	Acacia	Seed w/pod	1
# 333	**Hordeum vulgare*	Barley	Hull	Fragments
	*Ricinus communis	Castor bean	Seed	2 + fragments
	*Triticum dicoccum	Emmer wheat	Glume base	4
TS1b, Lv 7	**Acacia nilotica*	Acacia	Seed w/pod	6
SE Corner	**Triticum dicoccum*	Emmer wheat	Spikelet	1
#333				
TS1b, Lv 7	**cf. Buglossoides* sp.	Gromwell	Seed	1 + fragments
#347	*Citrullus lunatus*	Watermelon	Seed	2
	*Coriandrum sativum	Coriander	Capsule	1 fragment
	Cyperus esculentus	Sedge	Rhyzome	1
	Hordeum vulgare	Barley	Rachis	8
			Grain	2
	Linum usitatissimum	Flax	Capsule	Fragments
	*Lolium temulentum	Ryegrass	Grain	2
	Triticum dicoccum	Emmer wheat	Spikelet	31
			Glume base	15
			Internode	4
			Grain	1 fragment
			Glume	Fragments
TS1b, Removing	*Phoenix dactylifera*	Date	Seed	1
LV 5, #302				
TS1d, Lv 3	*Cordia myxa*	Egyptian plum	Fruit stone	3
Lot 1	*Mimusops schimperi*	Persea	Seed	22 + fragments
	Olea europaea	Olive	Fruit stone	2
	Phoenix dactylifera	Date	Seed	26
	Prunus persica	Peach	Fruit stone	1
	Triticum cf. *durum*	Naked wheat; cf. hard wheat	Internode	2
TS1d, #449	*Hordeum vulgare*	Barley	Grain	ca. 48
Lv 4, F 10			Rachis segment	15
			Hull	Hundreds of fragments
	Lathyrus aphaca	Yellow vetchling	Seed	1
	Linum usitatissimum	Flax	Capsule	Fragments

PROVENIENCE	LATIN NAME	COMMON NAME	PLANT PART	NUMBER
	Lolium temulentum	Ryegrass	Grain	10
	Medicago hispida	Medick	Seed	2
	Triticum dicoccum	Emmer wheat	Spikelet	ca. 250
			Glume	Hundreds of fragments
	Triticum cf. *durum*	Naked wheat; cf. hard wheat	Rachis segment	7
			Glume	Hundreds of fragments
	Triticum sp.	Wheat	Grain	4
	cf. *Vicia ervilia*	Grass pea	Testa	Fragments
TS2, Lv 2	*Hordeum vulgare*	Barley	Rachis segment	2
			Grain	3
	Phalaris paradoxa	Canary grass	Grain	2
	Triticum dicoccum	Emmer wheat	Glume	1 fragment
TS2, Lv 2 SWQ	*Mimusops schimperi*	Persea	Seed	1
	Phoenix dactylifera	Date	Seed	1
TS2, Lv 2 SEQ, #505	*Phoenix dactylifera*	Date	Seed	1
TS2, Lv 2 NWQ Fill above Floor of Structure A #514	*Phoenix dactylifera*	Date	Seed	647
TS2, Lv 2 NEQ	*Triticum dicoccum*	Emmer wheat	Spikelet	1
TS2, Lv 2 F 2, NEQ	*Hordeum vulgare*	Barley	Rachis segment	1
			Grain	1
Material on top of floor	*Phoenix dactylifera*	Date	Seed	13
TS2, Lv 3 SEQ, #526	*Phoenix dactylifera*	Date	Seed	2
TS2, Lv 4 Lot 2	*Phoenix dactylifera*	Date	Seed	12
TS2, Lv 5 SWQ, #554	*Triticum dicoccum*	Emmer wheat	Glume base	2
TS2, Lv 5 B F 10	*Triticum dicoccum*	Emmer wheat	Glume base	1
			Glume	1 fragment
TS2, Lv 5 F 12, #561	*Hyphaene thebaica*	Dom	Mesocarp	1
TS2, Lv 5 F 12 A, #544	*Citrullus colocynthus*	Watermelon	Seed	1
	Phoenix dactylifera	Date	Seed	1

PROVENIENCE	LATIN NAME	COMMON NAME	PLANT PART	NUMBER
	Triticum cf. *durum*	Naked wheat; cf. hard wheat	Rachis segment	1
TS2, Lv 5-6 F 8	*Phoenix dactylifera*	Date	Seed	1
TS2, Lv 6 Lot 1	*Phoenix dactylifera*	Date	Seed	1
TS2, Lv 6 Lot 2, #313	**Citrullus lunatus*	Watermelon	Seed	2
	*Hordeum vulgare	Barley	Grain	2
	*Triticum dicoccum	Emmer wheat	Spikelet	1
TS2, Lv 8 Lot 1A	*Triticum dicoccum*	Emmer wheat	Complete spikelet	77
TS2, Lv 9 Lot 1A, #597	*Cyperus* sp.	Sedge	Stem	1 fragment
TS2, NEQ #512	*Phoenix dactylifera*	Date	Seed	2
TS2, NEQ Level below floor - 167 cm	**Hordeum vulgare*	Barley	Internode	1
	Hyphaene thebaica	Dom	Mesocarp w/stone	1
	*Triticum dicoccum	Emmer wheat	Glume	Fragments
TS2, NEQ Just above floor- 167 cm below top of SW wall of Lot 3 #584	*Phoenix dactylifera*	Date	Seed	1
TS2, NEQ Floor 167 cm below top of Wall 3, #585	*Hordeum vulgare*	Barley	Internode	1
	Mimusops schimperi	Persea	Kernel	1
	Triticum dicoccum	Emmer wheat	Spikelet	2

V. The Plant Remains

TABLE 5.2
Stratigraphic Distribution of Plant Remains

	Emmer Wheat a) Rachis Fragment	b) Spikelet	c) Grain	Barley a) Rachis Fragment	b) Grain	Durum Wheat Rachis Fragment	Olive Stone	Flax a) Seed	b) Capsule	Castor Bean Seed	Sesame Capsule	Date Seed	Dom Fruit	Egyptian Plum Stone	Persea Seed	Peach Stone	Watermelon Seed	Balanites Stone
TS-1-1							2+F					31+F			1			
TS-1-2																		
TS-1-3	2F					2	2					45+F		3	22+F	3+F		
TS-1-4	100s	ca. 250		16	ca. 48	20			F						1+F			
TS-1-5		1		1		5	ca. 17		1			154+F		10+F	12+F	15+F		1
TS-1-6		2					5					124			1			1
TS-1-7	28	35	F	12	2+F	1		F		8+F	F	16	1		1		3+F	
TS-1-8																		
TS-1-9																		
TS-1-10							1					35		1				1
TS-1-11					F		3+F					31+F			F	5		
TS-1-12					F	F							F					
TS-1-13																		
TS-2-1																		
TS-2-2		1+F		3	4							662			1			
TS-2-3												2						
TS-2-4												12						
TS-2-5		F				1						2	1				1	
TS-2-6		1			2							1					2	
TS-2-7																		
TS-2-8		77																
TS-2-9																		
TS-2-12		2+F		2								3	1		1			

F = Fragment(s).

TABLE 5.2 (continued)

	Christ's Thorn Stone	Carob Seed	Sycamore Fig Fruit	Coriander Capsule	Pine Scale	cf. Bittervetch	Sedge a) Rhyzome	Sedge b) Stem	Acacia Seed and Pod	Ryegrass Seed	Canary Grass Seed	Medick Seed	Yellow Vetchling Seed	Vetch (V. lutea) Seed	cf. Gromwell Seed
TS-1-1															
TS-1-2															
TS-1-3															
TS-1-4						F				10		2	1		
TS-1-5	1	5		F	F							1			
TS-1-6										2				1	
TS-1-7			1	F			3		8	2	1				1+F
TS-1-8															
TS-1-9															
TS-1-10															
TS-1-11															
TS-1-12															
TS-1-13															
TS-2-1															
TS-2-2											2				
TS-2-3															
TS-2-4															
TS-2-5															
TS-2-6															
TS-2-7															
TS-2-8															
TS-2-9							F								
TS-2-12															

VI. THE TEXTILES

DIANA RYESKY

University of Washington, Seattle

The excavations at el-Hibeh yielded over 550 samples of textiles, massed fibers, basketry, and cordage. We conducted a preliminary analysis of these materials at the University of Washington during May, 1982, with the primary objectives of describing these textiles and assessing their distribution through the stratigraphic sequence.[1]

A. Procedures

We began by providing each piece with an identification number and temporary storage. Our first procedure was to transfer the fabrics and fibers from the plastic site collection bags to cardboard boxes. Each box contains the textile fragments recovered from one specific provenience within the site. The boxes were assigned consecutive numbers from one to 114. We grouped together fragments that, upon initial examination of weave structure, yarn structure, and weave density, appeared to be part of the same textile. The term "piece," which herein denotes like fragments grouped together, is the unit of analysis in this study. A piece may consist of one fragment or of many fragments. Each piece within each box received a consecutive number beginning with one; used in combination with its box number (e.g. B12 P2), each piece has an individual identity and is easily retrievable. Some boxes contain only one piece, while others have as many as thirty-six. Storage for pieces consists of small plastic bags with piece and box numbers written on them. Bags are loosely stored, unsealed, in lidded and numbered boxes. As soon as possible, we intend to arrange permanent storage for these materials.

Only the textiles selected for photography were relaxed and minimally cleaned, using M. Burnham's (1975) procedure. A sumi brush was used to remove excess dust from the textiles. If dyed, solubility was tested by rubbing the textiles with a Q-tip soaked with distilled water. The textiles were then placed on a glass surface and sprayed with distilled water until quite wet. Excess moisture was removed with blotter paper, and folds were

[1] The author wishes to thank several people for their generous assistance in various aspects of this study. Janet Newby, Dona Rozanski, and Susan Torntore, students in the Division of Textile Science and Costume Studies, with competence, ideas and enthusiasm, aided in the analysis and cleaning of the artifacts and with the photography. Robert Wenke's contribution to all aspects of the planning and execution of this study is greatly appreciated. He is responsible for the computer programming and he offered helpful comments on an earlier draft of this paper. Susan Torntore took most of the photographs.

carefully manipulated flat. Textiles received a maximum of two sprayings and blottings. Once dry, gentle probing beneath them with a dissecting needle loosened them from the glass. Although much dirt came out of the textiles onto the blotter paper, this procedure did not leave them clean.

B. The Samples

The artifacts analyzed here represent approximately 95 percent of the textile remains recovered from el-Hibeh. The 574 study pieces include 384 woven textiles (67 percent); 121 pieces of massed fibers (21 percent); sixty-five of cordage (11 percent) and four of basketry (1 percent).

The cordage, basketry, and massed fibers received no further analysis at this time; however some of this material will be described briefly. The cordage samples appear to be manufactured from unidentified hard fibers as well as from fibers such as those used in the woven textiles. Cordage specimens range in diameter from approximately 1 mm to 1.1 cm (Plate 6.1). Massed fibers consist of 1) puffs of fibrous material; 2) felted fibers; 3) flexible yarns knotted or grouped together (some of these could be textiles in an extreme state of disintegration) and 4) yarn wound in packages (perhaps flattened balls) (Plate 6.2; Table 6.1).

C. Data Analysis

Considerations in setting up procedures for data analysis included time availability (the textiles arrived in Seattle only a month before the final report was due), the fragile nature of textile artifacts, the large quantity of material, and our desire to describe the composition of this assemblage of textiles in such a way as to facilitate comparisons with other excavated materials. Thus, variables selected for study encompass only ones which could be observed and accurately documented from the textiles in the unrelaxed condition in which they came from the excavation. The variables chosen include yarn structure, fiber content, weave structure, weave density, color, and decoration. This information was coded for analysis by computer. Comments about other details such as sewing and selvages were written on the coding forms. Virtually all of the textiles from el-Hibeh consist of fragments; selvages were observed on only 4 percent of the pieces. Therefore in most cases in this preliminary analysis we have not attempted to distinguish between warp and weft (see King 1978:90).[2]

Yarn structures encountered include pieces made entirely of Z spun single yarns; of S spun singles; of Z spun, S plied yarns; or of S spun, S plied yarns. Other categories include fabrics that have S spun singles in one set of elements and plied threads in the other set. In these cases, the most frequent plying technique is Z spun, S plied. Also, some textiles exhibit S spun singles in one set of elements and Z spun single yarns in the other. S spun single yarn used throughout a textile is the type most often encountered at el-Hibeh (70

---

[2] This paper contains a glossary which defines the weaving terms used here.

percent). The next most common yarn structure is where S spun single yarns appear in one set of elements while plied yarns occur in the other set (15 percent; Table 6.2).

Microscopic fiber analysis was conducted on forty pieces randomly selected from the excavations. We chose only one fiber sample per piece and at this time did not investigate the possibility that a textile could contain more than one type of fiber. Slides were made, using mineral oil as a wetting agent. Longitudinal views of these fibers were compared to modern fiber samples, to the standards given in the *Technical Manual* of the American Association of Textile Chemists and Colorists (1979), and to photomicrographs of archaeological fibers from Nubia (Mayer-Thurman and Williams 1979:50-51). The fibers fit into the categories of linen, cotton, wool, and unknown bast. Much of the wool was badly degraded; and, given the possibility of modern hair fibers differing from ancient ones, we could not determine from which animal (sheep, goat, camel) the wool derived, with the technique being utilized. More sophisticated techniques of fiber analysis might provide greater specificity as to the nature of the wools. Linen makes up 52 percent (twenty-one) of the fibers analyzed; 38 percent are wool; 8 percent, cotton; and 2 percent, unknown bast (Table 6.3).

The predominant weave structure, occurring in 94 percent of the pieces, is 1/1 plain weave. Another 5 percent consists of plain weave variants (2/1 and 2/2), and 1 percent includes tapestry, supplementary weft, plaiting or twining, and knotting (Table 6.4). The 1/1 plain weaves vary tremendously in terms of yarn diameter and warps and wefts per centimeter. To give an idea of the variety encountered in these weaves, we measured these variables on the pieces selected and relaxed for photography. Since, at this stage of analysis, warp and weft were not determined, the set of elements containing fewer units was assumed to be the warp. Warp counts range from 3 to 28 per cm with a mean of 11, while weft counts run from 8 to 40 per cm and have a mean of 20. The coarsest textile has 3 warps and 8 wefts per cm, while the finest one contains 28 warps and 29 wefts. The mean yarn diameter for both elements is .7 mm but in the warp, diameters range from .2 mm to 1.2 mm and in the weft, from .15 mm to 2.0 mm (Plates 6.3 and 6.4).

A rough visual measure of weave density determined if the weave is balanced or faced. The category of faced weaves includes structures where one element totally covers the other, as well as where one element tends to dominate over the other. Textiles in which the weave varies from balanced to faced were coded with the category that predominates. Just over half the pieces have balanced weaves (Table 6.5).

Certain special weave structures merit comment. Only one piece of tapestry weave (B82 P4) occurs in the sample. Its discontinuous wefts exhibit dovetailed joins and it has 13 warps, 26 ground wefts, and 30 pattern wefts per cm (Plate 6.5). A small beige cotton fragment contains tiny decorative lozenges in what is probably discontinuous supplementary weft (B70 P3; Plate 6.6). Yet another piece appears to be either plaited or twined: pairs of wool yarns seem to twist around each other in rows, but it is difficult to determine if a warp-weft system is present because, also, many yarns move in eccentric paths. A geometric pattern is formed utilizing open areas of the textile. Since the brittle yarns still retain a great deal of dirt that obscures examination of the structure, further investigation must await cleaning and stabilization of the textile (B53 P30; Plate 6.7). Also, one specimen consists of cords that are knotted together in a netlike way (B31 P1; Plate 6.8). Techniques that produce texture on a plain weave surface include use of some tightly spun yarns along with looser twisted ones (B33 P1; Plate 6.9).

In the course of examination of the unrelaxed specimens, selvages were found on fifteen of the 384 pieces (4 percent). Some selvages have two warps interacting with one weft on the very edge of the fabric, even though the rest of the textile contains 1/1 plain weave (B77 P30; Plate 6.4). Other selvages, heavily corded, are constructed by using three units of five warps each on the edge. As the weft emerges from the balanced 1/1 plain weave, it moves to the edge of the fabric, back only through the three groups of five warps, back to the edge, and then makes a complete weft pick. This permits the weft to cover almost completely the warp units along the edge (B44 P4; Plate 6.3).

Four fringed pieces came to light. Analysis suggests that the fringe probably is made from four S spun warp threads knotted together, then Z plied and final plied S. Doubled wefts occur in the five rows just before the fringe begins (B35 P26; Plate 6.10).

Stitching occurs on 5 percent (twenty) of the pieces. Several pieces have seams; most, however, contain rolled hems stitched with large stitches and coarse thread (B84 P14; Plate 6.11). Only one piece exhibits shaping through sewing; it is folded and has a seam up part of one side (B52 P1; Plate 6.12).

Colors were coded using colloquial color terms. Since the textiles remained dirty, it seemed inappropriate to use a Munsell system to categorize them. Some code inconsistencies occurred between beige, brown, and grey, between brown and purple, and between beige and yellow. The pieces that received minimal cleaning for photography brightened considerably, making some of these color differences more readily apparent.

Beige is the predominant color of the el-Hibeh textiles; 72 percent of the textile pieces are completely beige. Plain brown textiles make up 4 percent of the total. Some textiles were dyed yellow (8 percent), while plain blue, red, green and purple textiles together make up about 5 percent of the total. Textiles exhibiting more than one color form just 10 percent of the total. About half of the multicolored group (seventeen) consist of striped items; others have warps of one color and wefts of another, two colors used in alternate sheds of the warp (B97 P2; Plate 6.13), or they are stained. All multicolored pieces exhibit either beige or yellow in combination with another color (Table 6.6).

Decoration occurs in just 5 percent of the pieces. Most decoration consists of stripes; one textile, the tapestry piece, has a motif in the form of two stepped triangles (B82 P4; Plate 6.5) and lozenges appear on a cotton fragment as supplementary elements (B70 P3; Plate 6.6). Striped textiles usually have backgrounds of yellow or beige with stripes in purple, blue, or black. On a few pieces, stripes occur in closely spaced groupings (B50 P3; Plate 6.4; B52 P1, Plate 6.12); however, most stripes appear singly and widely spaced on the fabric (B33 P1, Plate 6.9; B44 P9, Plate 6.3). Stripes range in width from approximately 3 mm to 1 cm. Selvage information presently available indicates that stripes tend to occur in the weft direction (B33 P1; Plate 6.9) although warp striping also appears (B50 P3; Plate 6.4).[3] Further analysis of decorative elements indicates that 70 percent of the stripes are faced, that stripes almost always occur in 1/1 plain weave structures, and that 59 percent of the time they are placed on faced backgrounds.

In this preliminary analysis, little can be inferred about the function of the textiles

---

[3] In textile terminology, the word stripe indicates parallel lines of color in the warp direction and the word band denotes the same but in the weft direction (Burnham 1980:2,136). In this preliminary study, since warp and weft usually cannot be distinguished, the word "stripe" is used.

found at el-Hibeh. However, the presence of plain weaves that vary from very coarse to very fine implies that fabrics were planned and woven for different functions (Plates 6.3, 6.4). Fringed edges and curved hemmed edges suggest possible use on garments (Plates 6.10, 6.11). Narrow bands may be edgings or straps (Plate 6.13). Also, some textiles are tied in knots for some unknown purpose. The knotted cordage suggests fish net (B31 P1; Plate 6.8). In addition, some textiles exhibit extreme discoloration and brittleness from chemical changes, perhaps from being used in the process of mummification. Also, one textile encloses the remains of a small lizard (Plate 6.14).

The next stage of our preliminary analysis involved a computer based cross-tabulation of weave structure, weave density, fiber content, and yarn structure. When weave structure is compared with weave density, it shows that plain weave variants strongly tend to be balanced. However, 1/1 plain weaves are about equally divided between balanced and faced structures (Table 6.7). In comparing yarn structure with weave density, S singles appear in a greater proportion of faced weaves (78 percent) than of balanced weaves (65 percent) and balanced weaves are slightly more likely (18 percent) than faced ones (11 percent) to contain single yarns spun S in one set of elements and plied threads in the other set (Table 6.8).

A cross-tabulation of yarn structure with weave structure shows that 86 percent of the non-1/1 plain weaves contain S spun yarns while 1/1 plain weaves exhibit a greater variation in types of yarns used (Table 6.9).

Fiber content demonstrates strong correlations with aspects of yarn structure and weave density. Strikingly, all the wool yarns are S spun singles, while two of the three cotton pieces consist of Z spun threads and the other has Z spun yarns in one set of elements. Linen exhibits the greatest variety of yarn treatment and combination in fabrics; 71 percent of the time it occurs as S spun singles; plied yarns and S singles combined with plied yarns are used in the remainder of the pieces (Table 6.10). Clearly, definite patterns of spinning are associated with each fiber. Bellinger (1950) indicates that the linen fiber's naturally occurring S twist leads most cultures to spin it that way. Such habits may have carried over, in Egypt, to wool. Also, plying only occurs on linen; whether the initial twist is S or Z, the final plying direction is always S. In addition, Bellinger's research suggests that cotton fibers, when spun Z (as are most of el-Hibeh's cottons), tend to hold up better when washed.

As for weave density, cotton only occurs in balanced weaves. Linen and wool, however, show no difference in terms of being used in balanced or faced weaves (Table 6.11).

D. Comparisons Between the Two Test Squares Excavated at el-Hibeh

Of the 384 textiles retrieved in the excavations at el-Hibeh, eighty-two pieces or 21 percent came from Test Square 2 (hereafter TS2) while the remaining 79 percent (302 pieces) were found in Test Square 1 (TS1; Table 6.12 presents a breakdown of the textiles found in each level and quadrant of the site). As discussed above, the contents of TS1's lower levels may be roughly contemporary with much of TS2, which consists chiefly of building fill (p. 36). In order to examine change in textile variables over time at el-Hibeh, we will compare TS2 in its entirety with TS1 broken down by excavation level (but not divided by quadrants). Thus, TS1 will be split into three groupings: LEVELS 1 to 3; LEVELS 4 to 6; and LEVELS 7 to 12.

Greater diversity in weave structure appears in later time periods in the site, at least as is reflected in our rather small samples of excavated deposits. TS2 contained only 1/1 plain woven textiles with the exception of one textile. TS1 held the other 23 non-1/1 plain woven pieces. In fact, in TS1, non-1/1 plain weaves make up 2 percent of the total in the lower levels, but increase to 12 percent in the uppermost strata (Table 6.13).

Balanced weaves comprise about half the textiles in TS2 and a somewhat larger proportion of those in TS1 (Table 6.14).

Of the forty textiles randomly sampled for fiber analysis, twenty-seven came from TS1 and thirteen from TS2. Cotton makes up 23 percent (three) of the fibers analyzed for TS2, while it did not occur at all in TS1. Wool appears in only 8 percent of the textiles from TS2, while its use dramatically increases over time in TS1 (from 14 percent to 64 percent). Linen and other bast fibers occur in 70 percent of the pieces analyzed from TS2; in TS1, their use decreases over time from 86 percent to 36 percent. Thus, cotton and linen appear to have been more prevalent in earlier periods of the site, while wool became more important in later times—all inferences based on insufficient data, it must be stressed (Table 6.15).

The unexpected occurrence of cotton in TS2, the earlier test square, raises some questions requiring further research. The cotton pieces came from LEVELS 1 and 2, which concern the remains of a later building set over an earlier filled structure (p. 30). Thus, these cottons may be as old or older than the most ancient known cotton textile fragments in the area, all roughly contemporary with Roman times. These include fragments found at Semna South (Brandford 1977:9), Ballana, and Qustul in Nubia, and those encountered at Karanog and Meroë (Mayer-Thurman and Williams 1979:37). Furthermore, the el-Hibeh cotton textiles differ from those of Ballana and Qustul in that the el-Hibeh material has two to three times more warps and wefts per centimeter; it has predominantly Z spun yarns as opposed to the S spun ones occurring in Nubia; and yarn diameter seems, from the photographs, to be much larger in Nubia (Mayer-Thurman and Williams 1979: plates). Some of the Semna South cottons approach the el-Hibeh material in thread count, but they too are S spun (Brandford 1977). It is presently thought that cotton is of fairly recent introduction in Egypt, although it was known in the Indus Valley since the 3rd millennium B.C. Also, evidence exists for cotton plants in Nubia from about 3100 B.C., and it may have been imported into Egypt from cotton-producing areas in Hellenistic times (Forbes 1956:48; Mayer-Thurman and Williams 1979:37).

Yarn structures show some differentiation between the two test squares. S spun yarns occur in 65 percent of the pieces in TS2. In the lower levels of TS1, they make up about 48 percent of the total and then greatly increase in proportion through time. Eleven percent of the pieces in TS2 have S spun elements in one direction and plied ones in the other set. At the bottom levels of TS1, this type of yarn usage suddenly increases, only to decrease again through time. Also, Z spun fibers occur more frequently in TS2 than in TS1. These data, as well as previous cross-tabulations, suggest that yarn structure may be related to changes in fibers being used (Table 6.16).

Dyes appear more frequently in TS1 than in TS2. In TS2, only blue, black, and green occur, whereas in TS1 the palette grows to include yellow, red, and purple. In general, color occurrence in the lower levels of TS1 is similar to that of TS2, and dyes appear much more often in TS1's more recent strata (Table 6.17). The growth of the color palette is concurrent with an increased usage of wool.

Decoration on textiles, in this case mostly stripes, occurs in about the same proportion of textiles in TS1 as in TS2 (4 to 6 percent; Table 6.18).

E. Summary and Conclusions

Even though only a few variables from small samples of the many textiles deposited at el-Hibeh have been analyzed in this preliminary study, several patterns begin to emerge which should receive further testing. First, variation in textile technique over time at el-Hibeh may be related to changing fiber use—from linen to a greater emphasis on wool. Our data on yarn structure and dye use seem to correlate with Bellinger's idea (1950) that different techniques and technologies respond to the nature and flexibility of the fibers being utilized or to pre-existing culture patterns (Wild 1970:44). Secondly, the preliminary analysis of the textile variables suggests, as in the pottery sequence, that the textiles in TS2 show similarities to those in lower levels of TS1. These trends, as well as other dating information from the site, should be correlated with historical data which indicate, for example, that efforts to improve wool production took place during Hellenistic times (Forbes 1956: 14,236).

It is well known that textile production was an important aspect of the Egyptian economy in the Islamic period. Linguistic information such as the abundance of words indicating various types, functions, and qualities of linen suggests the importance of both the weaving industry and of cloth in the life of the Egyptians in earlier times as well (Forbes 1956:42-43). Also, during Hellenistic and Roman periods, both linen and wool textiles were produced, sometimes in workshops, sometimes in homes, for local use and for export. There was much governmental regulation of these industries (Forbes 1956:39-40,236-238). Further analysis of the textiles from el-Hibeh should relate the assemblage to what is known from historical documents about the nature and scope of weaving industries and the importance of cloth in Egyptian trade.

Pottery and lithics, which occur widely and preserve well over time, have served as the basis for the development of much of the methodology for the analysis of change over time in artifacts. Textiles, rarely encountered in excavations because they only are preserved under very specific climatic conditions, often are not thoroughly studied and adequately conserved even if they are recovered. Also, our knowledge of textiles in the regions where they are preserved tends to be skewed towards the decorated ones because they attract the attention of grave robbers, they reach collectors as art objects, and they are the ones most readily analyzed through stylistic methods. For ancient Egypt and Nubia, a growing body of information that systematically describes textile remains includes Brookner's (1979) analysis of decorated textiles and Eastwood's (1982) discussion and catalogue, both dealing with Quseir al-Qadim; Brandford's thorough report (1977) on the Semna South material; Mayer-Thurman and Williams' analytical catalogue of the Ballana and Qustul finds (1979); and Bergman's (1975) study of Nubian textiles.

Future detailed and quantitative studies of the el-Hibeh materials, then, should examine the many variables involved in textile construction. Warp and weft count ratios as well as density and face ratios of el-Hibeh's plain weaves, as suggested and used by Wallace (1975) in a study of pre-Columbian Peruvian plain weaves, may yield information on trends over time. It is possible that the variability in textiles is as sensitive an indicator of time as are pottery styles. In the few cases in which they do remain preserved in excavations, their characteristics should be as completely and systematically analyzed as are those of ceramics.

Glossary

BALANCED WEAVE: the warp and weft elements are equally spaced and approximately the same in size and flexibility (Emery 1966:76).

DIRECTION OF TWIST: designates whether the trend of the spiral of the twisted elements of a yarn conforms, when held in a vertical position, to the central portion of the letter S or Z (Emery 1966:11).

DOVETAILING: a type of tapestry join in which discontinuous wefts turn back alternately around the warp which is their common boundary (Emery 1966:80).

FACED WEAVE: the warp and weft are not equally spaced and one element obscures the other from view.

PLAIN WEAVE: each weft unit passes alternately under and over successive warp units with each reversing the process of the one before it. Variants of plain weave always maintain the simple alternating order of interlacing (Emery 1966:76). Variants present in this study include:

> 1/1 plain weave: warp and weft units consist of one thread each.
> 2/1 plain weave: one set of elements has two threads per unit while the other has just one.
> 2/2 plain weave: both sets of elements have two threads per unit.

PLIED YARNS: occur when two or more single yarns are twisted together (Emery 1966: 10). Usually, but not always, yarns are plied in the opposite direction to that in which they are spun; i.e., if they are spun Z they usually are plied S.

SELVAGE: the longitudinal edge of a textile enclosed with weft loops; it may be distinguished from the rest of the fabric by warp threads differing from those in the body of the textile and sometimes by a change in the interlacing (Burnham 1980:116).

SINGLE YARN: one in which the fibers have been spun in one direction or the other; it is the simplest continuous aggregate of spun fibers suitable for fabric construction (Emery 1966:9). These are sometimes called spun or twisted yarns, as opposed to plied ones.

TAPESTRY WEAVE: weft faced plain weave using discontinuous wefts, usually of different colors, to produce a pattern.

WARP: the longitudinal threads of a textile; the ones placed on the loom (Burnham 1980: 170).

WEFT: a textile's transverse threads; those that are passed through the sheds (Burnham 1980:179).

TABLE 6.1

Distribution of Textile Remains
By Excavation Unit and Level

EXCAVATION UNITS

TYPES OF TEXTILE REMAINS	TS1 LEVELS			TS2 LEVELS	TOTAL
	1-3	4-6	7-12		
Woven textiles	66% (126)	55% (78)	75% (98)	76% (82)	67% (384)
Basketry	- (1)	1% (1)	- (0)	2% (2)	1% (4)
Cordage	13% (25)	14% (20)	11% (14)	6% (65)	11% (65)
Massed fibers	21% (40)	31% (44)	14% (19)	17% (18)	21% (121)
	100% (192)	101% (143)	100% (131)	101% (108)	100% (574)

TABLE 6.2

Yarn Structure: Frequencies

YARN STRUCTURE	%	N
Z singles	5	18
S singles	70	269
Z spun S plied	1	4
S spun S plied	5	18
S, plied*	15	57
S,Z**	4	15
Unidentified	1	3
TOTAL	101%	384

*S singles in one set of elements and plied yarns in the other.
**S singles in one set of elements and Z singles in the other.

TABLE 6.3

Fiber: Frequencies

FIBER	%	N
Cotton	8	3
Linen	52	21
Wool	38	15
Unknown bast	2	1
TOTAL	100%	40

TABLE 6.4

Weave Structure: Frequencies

WEAVE STRUCTURE	%	N
Plain weave 1/1	94	360
Plain weave 2/1	3	9
Plain weave 2/2	2	8
Others	1	
Tapestry		1
Twined or plaited		1
Other plain weave variant		1
Unidentified		2
TOTAL	100	384

TABLE 6.5

Weave Density: Frequencies

WEAVE DENSITY	%	N
Balanced	55	212
Faced	44	169
Unidentified	1	3
TOTAL	100%	384

TABLE 6.6

Colors and Color Combinations: Frequency Distributions

PIECES HAVING ONE COLOR:	%*	N
Beige	72	275
Blue	3	13
Red	1	5
Yellow	8	30
Green	1	3
Brown	4	17
Gray	-	2
Purple	-	1
SUB-TOTAL	90%	346

*All percentages based on N=383.

PIECES HAVING MORE THAN ONE COLOR:	%	N
Beige/black	1	3
Beige/blue	1	4
Beige/red	1	3
Beige/green	-	1
Beige/brown	5	18
Beige/purple	-	1
Yellow/brown	-	3
Yellow/purple	1	4
SUB-TOTAL	10%	37
TOTAL	100%	383

TABLE 6.7

Weave Density By Weave Structure

WEAVE STRUCTURE

WEAVE DENSITY	PLAIN 1/1		PLAIN WEAVE VARIANTS (2/1,2/2, other)		TAPESTRY	
Balanced	54%	(196)	80%	(16)	-	(0)
Faced	46%	(164)	20%	(4)	100%	(1)
TOTAL	100%	(360)	100%	(20)	100% (1) = 381*	

*Three unidentified textiles not included in this table.

TABLE 6.8

Yarn Structure By Weave Density

WEAVE DENSITY

YARN STRUCTURE	BALANCED		FACED		UNIDENTIFIED
Z singles	6%	(12)	4%	(6)	
S singles	65%	(137)	78%	(131)	(1)
plied	7%	(14)	5%	(8)	
S, plied*	18%	(38)	11%	(19)	
S, Z**	5%	(10)	3%	(5)	
Unidentified	-	(1)	-	(0)	(2)
TOTAL	101%	(121)	101%	(169)	(3) = 384

*S singles in one set of elements and plied yarns in the other set.

**S singles in one set of elements and Z singles in the other set.

TABLE 6.9

Yarn Structure By Weave Structure

YARN STRUCTURE		WEAVE STRUCTURE			
	1/1 PLAIN WEAVE		OTHER WEAVE STRUCTURES		UNIDENTIFIED
Z singles	5%	(17)	4%	(1)	
S singles	69%	(250)	86%	(19)	
Plied	6%	(21)	4%	(1)	
S, plied*	16%	(56)	4%	(1)	
S,Z**	4%	(15)	-	(0)	
Unidentified	-	(1)	-	(0)	(2)
TOTAL	100%	(360)	98%	(22)	(2) = 384

*S singles in one set of elements and plied yarns in the other set.
**S singles in one set of elements and Z singles in the other set.

TABLE 6.10

Yarn Structure By Fiber

YARN STRUCTURE			FIBER					
	COTTON		LINEN		WOOL		UNKNOWN BAST	
Z singles	66%	(2)	-	(0)	-	(0)		
S singles	-	(0)	71%	(15)	100%	(15)	100%	(1)
Z spun S plied	-	(0)	5%	(1)	-	(0)		
S spun S plied	-	(0)	14%	(3)	-	(0)		
S, plied*	-	(0)	10%	(2)	-	(0)		
S,Z**	34%	(1)	-	(0)	-	(0)		
TOTAL	100%	(3)	100%	(21)	100%	(15)	100%	(1) = 40

*S singles in one set of elements and plied yarns in the other set.
**S singles in one set of elements and Z singles in the other set.

TABLE 6.11

Weave Density By Fiber

WEAVE DENSITY			FIBER						
	COTTON		LINEN		WOOL		UNKNOWN BAST		
Balanced	100%	(3)	62%	(13)	60%	(9)	-	(0)	
Faced	-	(0)	38%	(8)	40%	(6)	100%	(1)	
TOTAL	100%	(3)	100%	(21)	100%	(15)	100%	(1) = 40	

TABLE 6.12

Distribution of Textile Pieces

		PROVENIENCE			
		TS1			TS2
LEVEL	1a	1b	1d		
1	0	67	0	6	
2	0	0	0	16	
3	2	39	18	6	
4	2	3	1	4	
5	43	5	2	32	
6	9	13	0	2	
7	11	73	0	2	
8	1	0	0	1	
9	0	0	0	0	
10	7	0	0	0	
11	3	0	1	15	
12	2	0	0	0	
TOTAL	80	200	22	82	= 384

TABLE 6.13

**Distribution of Weave Structures by
Excavation Unit and Level**

WEAVE STRUCTURE		EXCAVATION UNIT			
		TS1 LEVELS			TS2
	1-3	4-6	7-12		
Plain 1/1	88% (111)	92% (72)	98% (96)	99% (81)	
Others	12% (12)	8% (6)	2% (2)	1% (1)	
TOTAL	100% (126)	100% (78)	100% (98)	100% (82) = 384	

TABLE 6.14

**Distribution of Weave Density by
Excavation Unit and Level**

WEAVE DENSITY		EXCAVATION UNIT			
		TS1 LEVELS			TS2
	1-3	4-6	7-12		
Balanced	56% (70)	49% (38)	65% (64)	49% (40)	
Faced	44% (55)	50% (39)	35% (34)	50% (41)	
Unidentified	1% (1)	1% (1)	- (0)	1% (1)	
TOTAL	101% (126)	100% (78)	100% (98)	100% (82) = 384	

TABLE 6.15

**Distribution of Fiber by Excavation
Unit and Level**

FIBERS		EXCAVATION UNIT			
		TS1 LEVELS			TS2
	1-3	4-6	7-12		
Cotton	- (0)	- (0)	- (0)	23% (3)	
Linen	36% (4)	33% (3)	86% (6)	62% (8)	
Wool	64% (7)	67% (6)	14% (1)	8% (1)	
Unknown Bast	- (0)	- (0)	- (0)	8% (1)	
TOTAL	100% (11)	100% (9)	100% (7)	101% (13) = 40	

TABLE 6.16

**Distribution of Yarn Structure by Excavation
Unit and Level**

YARN STRUCTURE					EXCAVATION UNIT			
			TS1 LEVELS				TS2	
	1-3		4-6		7-12			
Z singles	3%	(4)	5%	(4)	-	(0)	12%	(10)
S singles	87%	(109)	77%	(60)	48%	(47)	65%	(53)
Plied	-	(0)	3%	(2)	14%	(14)	8%	(6)
S, plied*	6%	(7)	8%	(6)	36%	(35)	11%	(9)
S,Z**	5%	(6)	6%	(5)	1%	(1)	4%	(3)
Unidentifiable	-	(0)	1%	(1)	1%	(1)	1%	(1)
TOTAL	100%	(126)	100%	(78)	100%	(98)	101%	(82) = 384

*S singles in one set of elements and plied yarns in the other set.

**S singles in one set of elements and Z singles in the other set.

TABLE 6.17

**Distribution of Colors by
Excavation Unit and Level***

COLORS					EXCAVATION UNIT			
			TS1 LEVELS				TS2	
	1-3		4-6		7-12			
Beige	69%	(87)	80%	(62)	90%	(88)	86%	(70)
Gray	1%	(2)	1%	(1)	-	(0)	1%	(1)
Brown	5%	(6)	8%	(6)	16%	(16)	10%	(8)
Black	1%	(8)	-	(0)	-	(0)	4%	(3)
Blue	3%	(3)	5%	(4)	3%	(3)	9%	(7)
Red	3%	(4)	4%	(3)	1%	(1)	-	(0)
Yellow	23%	(29)	7%	(5)	1%	(1)	-	(0)
Green	1%	(1)	3%	(2)	-	(0)	1%	(1)
Purple	3%	(4)	3%	(2)	-	(0)	-	(0)
N in LEVEL		(126)		(78)		(98)		(82) = 384

*All percentages calculated to N of level. Some textiles contain more than one color; therefore, the column percentages do not add up to 100%.

TABLE 6.18

**Distribution of Decorated Textiles by
Excavation Unit and Level**

DECORATION						EXCAVATION UNIT		
	TS1 LEVELS						TS2	
	1-3		4-6		7-12			
Not decorated	93%	(117)	96%	(75)	99%	(97)	94%	(77)
Decorated	7%	(9)	4%	(3)	1%	(1)	6%	(5)
TOTAL	100%	(126)	100%	(78)	100%	(98)	100%	(82) = 384

VII. SUMMARY AND CONCLUSIONS

The archaeological data from the 1980 season at el-Hibeh have been presented here in some detail, and it remains to relate these data to the broader questions of historical analysis with which this study began.

The justification for addressing these issues here has less to do with the discoveries of the 1980 season than with aspirations of the el-Hibeh project, for we have only begun to compile the evidence with which to address larger issues. Yet the last decade has seen a welcome expansion in the application of modern archaeological methods in Egypt and there is some hope that eventually we will have sufficient data with which to consider seriously the explanation of Egyptian cultural history. The el-Hibeh data were collected with this possibility in mind. Thus although the el-Hibeh data, in and of themselves, may not greatly advance our understanding of any transformations of Egyptian culture history, it is unlikely that our understanding of these transformations will be much advanced unless we specify in advance of fieldwork the kinds of information needed and the theoretical framework within which these data are to be interpreted.

It is neither practical nor appropriate here to review the paradigmatic throes of modern archaeology (see Dunnell 1982 for a recent summary); suffice it to say that, although differing on many fundamental points, many archaeologists still consider it possible to analyze settlements like el-Hibeh on a level above that having solely to do with how these ancient Egyptians lived and what they wrote and made.

There is a common perception that general explanation of the Egyptian past can be undertaken, at least at the level of the fairly mechanical factors of cultural ecology that constitute the "functional" form of explanation in archaeology (e.g., Butzer 1976, 1982).

I have elsewhere argued (Wenke 1980) for an evolutionary form of explanation as a possible complement to functional forms of argument, and there is a continuing debate in archaeology about the terms and concepts of explanation in general (reviewed in Dunnell 1982).

To relate some of these issues of explanation to el-Hibeh, consider the "town problem." Many analysts have been impressed by the, apparently, non-urban character of Egyptian settlement patterns, at least in comparison to other early civilizations. Most analyses of this problem have focussed on the Pharaonic periods, but the explosive urbanism of the Ptolemaic and Islamic periods are as much a part of the "town problem" as is the character of earlier Pharaonic settlements: it is the whole history of human settlement in Egypt that requires explanation.

What moves discussion of this matter beyond the realm of simple comparative history is that towns and cities can be viewed, not simply as one of several variant "epiphenomena" of cultural evolution, but as particularly potent agents of cultural evolution. Robert McC. Adams, for example, has argued in the context of Mesopotamian urbanism that cities generate evolutionary changes, that although one can try to reconstruct supra-settlement political systems, "cities" tend to be the unit of analysis because they constitute "the most visible and enduring reality of social life" (1981:248). He has also added that they should remain the focal point of archaeological research and interpretation in the case of Mesopotamia.

But Mesopotamia's settlement history is, of course, much different from that of Egypt. What is the proper unit of analysis for the Egyptian archaeological record, and what kinds of analyses are appropriate?

In part the "town-problem" is more apparent than real, a result of orthogenic and typological thinking. From the perspective of the modern world, it is hard not to view the historical sequence of settlement patterns as an almost inevitable "evolution" to a more developed state, in which the superior qualities of Western-style urban arrangements simply took longer to be realized in some places than in others. Thus, the early urban centers of ancient Mesopotamia, the Indus floodplain, Mexico, China, and elsewhere have been viewed as the "natural" form—a form Egypt only achieved at a comparatively late date.

Probably a more realistic and useful perspective is one in which, rather than static categories like village, town, and city, we instead see settlement patterns as capable of assuming highly variable characteristics of overall population size, functional roles performed, and architectural arrangements, depending on many diverse ecological, economic, political, and other factors.

From this point of view, we might not expect much similarity between, for example, Mesopotamian and Egyptian settlement patterns until the political, economic, and other factors that dictate settlement form and distribution became somewhat similar.

To relate all this to the study of Egyptian settlement patterns, it seems evident that analyses of these patterns should begin with a specification of what kind of explanation one is attempting. Regarding the location of el-Hibeh, for example, it may well be, as various scholars have asserted, that the settlement owes its placement and form mainly to the fact that it commands an important part of the Nile just at the edge of a large administrative area. And, similarly, it may be an explanation of sorts to say that the Egyptian *nome* system developed as a way of ensuring administrative efficiency in a decentralized economy. But it must be recognized that such functional statements do not constitute evolutionary explanations—at least not of the form and power that many analysts of cultural processes seek (Dunnell 1980; Cohen 1981; Diener and Robkin 1978).

What, exactly, we shall have to do to provide an evolutionary explanation of Egyptian settlement patterns and general cultural history is not at all clear. It is a general proposition of science that analytical units should be constructed on the basis of theory, but we have no body of theory to tell us what units to construct.

There are, however, a few steps we might make in this direction. To begin with, it is the essence of evolutionary theory to focus on *variability*, rather than on static *types* (Dunnell 1980; Dunnell and Wenke 1979; Yoffee 1979). Thus, as noted above, in attempting to cast the problem of Egyptian settlement patterns in an evolutionary format, we should probably abandon the traditional nomenclature of "forts," entrepôts, etc.—except as convenient forms of expression. Until we have some sense of the variability involved in these types of settlement, they can be only weak analytical units.

Another potential evolutionary approach to the problem of explaining Egyptian culture history involves the concept of cultural trait transmission. It can be argued (Wenke 1980) that *the* distinguishing characteristic of complex societies is that they depend on the inter-dependent labors of many specialists (potters, priests, architects, etc.) for successful functioning. Since most of these specialists require prolonged training (trait-transmission) as well as centralized administration, cities, with their large and dense populations, provide ideal environments for reliable and rapid trait transmission (Dunnell 1981; Wenke 1980; Cavalli-sforza and Feldman 1981).

Thus we must consider the possibility that cities are not just one of many equally efficacious solutions to problems of organizing people and institutions. It is likely that cities, in fact, represent the most effective way of arranging peoples in complex ancient economics, given the technologies, demographics, and other circumstances of the ancient world.

But towns and cities also have costs. They tend to have many inhabitants who are administrators or specialists not directly participating in economic production and who must be supported by agricultural craftsmen. In periods of primitive technologies, those inhabitants of cities who were farmers and herders had to walk increasingly long distances to their fields as the size of the city grew and the number of inhabitants increased. In ancient economies transport costs were such a large part of the total price of any good that the costs of supporting a large city mainly on products collected over a wide rural area and brought to the city would have been a major limiting factor to urban growth.

Urbanization also has several less direct "costs." It is well-established that many of the most virulent diseases of mankind are density dependent and probably appeared along with the first cities, when population densities were sufficient to maintain a reservoir of infection. Cities also have tendencies to polarize communities by expressing continually and starkly such things as wealth differentials, resulting, according to some interpretations, in class conflicts, deviant behaviors, and a whole catalogue of psychological disabilities.

The point here is that cities must be viewed not as automatic steps on the universal progression of cultural evolution, or as ultimately the best way for people to arrange themselves across the landscape. Rather, in analyzing Egyptian settlement patterns we must see them as products of natural selection operating directly on variability. Religious and social considerations doubtless played a role in determining settlement patterns, but in the last analysis, it would seem likely that the most important determinants of settlement patterns are environmental, technological, and political in nature.

The poverty of this natural selection-based "explanation" of settlement patterns is apparent, however, when we ask *why* natural selection fixed certain forms of variability in the case of ancient Egyptian settlement patterns. At this point we must fall back on the traditional functional forms of explanation, stressing Egypt's relatively unpopulated and protecting desert margins, its necessarily dispersed agricultural system, the self-sufficiency and economic/ecological *redundancy* of most segments of the Nile Valley, and the capacious transportation artery provided by the Nile.

Clearly, we are presently far from a truly evolutionary and powerful account of Egyptian settlement pattern studies. And the primary virtue in this context of projects like the el-Hibeh investigations would seem to be to provide a carefully recovered set of data about a small sample of this settlement history—that is, the classic inductivist approach.

In addition to the problem of explaining and understanding Egyptian settlement patterns, this study has also raised a question concerning Egyptian archaeological artifact classifications. It seems appropriate here to reiterate the conclusion arrived at in an earlier section this report (pp. 36-38), that there may be a fundamental limitation on the effectiveness of traditional Egyptian artifact typologies. Briefly, artifact typologies are analytical units that, to be useful, should be created for a specific purpose, such as chronological seriation, analysis of community patterning, or description. Selection of variables for these different kinds of analyses and the construction of units should be done according to specific methods of attribute isolation and combination. But in traditional Egyptian usage, artifact types are usually constructed on the basis of many different attributes, all combined in rather informal fashion, without the benefit of testing against the expectations of the seriation model—or whatever model is presumed to account for the distribution of these attributes through time and space.

It may well be, as suggested earlier, that unit construction through paradigmatic classificatory systems and tests of the resulting attribute combinations against established empirical generalizations about artifact variability through time and space constitute a generally more effective approach to Egyptian classification than those presently in common use.

Another problem exemplified, but not solved, by the el-Hibeh project involves the scale of the Egyptian archaeological record. Throughout this report we have contrasted the tiny samples we recovered with the great bulk of el-Hibeh itself, and it is not necessary to repeat here these many lamentations about sample sizes and biases.

But the question remains: how can archaeologists interested in larger problems of political and economic change deal with an archaeological record so vast that less than one per cent will ever be compentently excavated? There has been much recent use in this context of regional surveys and surface collections in augmentation of excavations, but even these resulting data are far from what will be necessary to answer many important questions about the Egyptian past. Sites like el-Hibeh, especially—"ghastly charnel houses of murdered evidence"—to use Petrie's felicitous phrase, are not susceptible to systematic surface collection as a substitute for sustained excavations.

At present, this problem of scale is unsolved. Perhaps the best approach is to construct as rigorous and far-ranging a set of testable hypotheses as possible before and during archaeological fieldwork, and then to fit the results as precisely as possible to these larger issues of interpretation—never forgetting for an instant the ambiguities and tentativeness of our interpretations. And of course it is difficult to conceive of any important problems of significance that will not require for their solution a body of carefully amassed evidence. For twenty years archaeologists have warned against blind inductivism, but this does not mean that we should give up careful screening, three-dimensional location of excavation units, and other minima of modern field techniques.

If we can amass sufficiently precise information about the art, architecture, technology, and diet of the people of el-Hibeh and the hundreds of other sites of all periods of occupation of the Nile Valley, we can at least place our cultural reconstructions and search for general explanations on a sounder footing. It is within this kind of environmental, technological, and ecological framework that our search for higher levels of explanation and synthesis must begin.

APPENDIX I: THE CERAMICS

ROBERT WENKE and NANETTE PYNE
University of Washington, Seattle

Many of the issues involving the classification and seriation of the el-Hibeh pottery samples have already been discussed, and it remains here to illustrate and describe the pottery types used in this analysis.

The types described in this appendix are preliminary field-sortings, and it is hoped that a more complete analysis with locus-by-locus frequencies can be compiled and published at a later time. It will be particularly useful to analyze the el-Hibeh pottery in terms of the paradigmatic classificatory procedures outlined earlier in this volume, as well as in terms of the mechanical and chemical variables outlined by Bourriau (1981:14).

Munsell color-chart readings for each type are provided—although it has yet to be demonstrated that such information is particularly useful, given the great variation in color on and through each sherd.

Appendix I

TYPE	MUNSELL COLOR CHART READING	DESCRIPTION
100	10R 5/8	very fine sand temper, no vegetable temper; smooth exterior and interior (burnished?); very high fired; "Roman."
101	2.5YR 5.5/8	fine sand temper, no vegetable temper; even color throughout; very high fired.
102	10R 5/8	sand/grit temper, no vegetable temper; even color throughout; medium fired.
103	2.5YR 5/8	medium grit temper, some vegetable temper; orange slip on exterior and interior; "Roman."
104	2.5YR 4.5/4	sand temper, no vegetable temper; even color throughout; medium to high fired.
105	2.5YR 6/4	grit temper, little vegetable temper; medium fired; some examples of this type have a red wash around the rim or exterior incised decoration—the distinguishing characteristic, however, is shape.
106	2.5YR 5/6	sand temper, very little vegetable temper; black/grey core, reddish slip on interior and exterior; high fired.
107	10R 4/3	grit/sand temper, some vegetable temper; lighter color core; medium to high fired.
108	10R 4/8	sand/grit temper, vegetable temper; even color throughout; medium to high fired.
109	2.5YR 4.5/4	fine sand temper, little vegetable temper; even color throughout; very high fired.
110	2.5YR 4/4	sand temper, little vegetable temper; black core; high fired.
111	10R 4/6	sand temper, little vegetable temper; dark red slip on interior and exterior; high fired.
112	10R 6/4	vegetable/sand temper; grey core; high fired.
113	5YR 5.5/8	medium grit temper, some vegetable temper; even color with traces of burnishing or red slip on exterior and interior; medium to high fired.
114	10R 4/4	sand temper, little vegetable temper; grey/black core; very high fired.
115	2.5YR 5/6	grit temper, medium vegetable temper, many limestone inclusions; lighter color core; medium fired.
116	5YR 5/6	sand and grit temper, some vegetable temper, some limestone inclusions; plum colored core; medium fired.

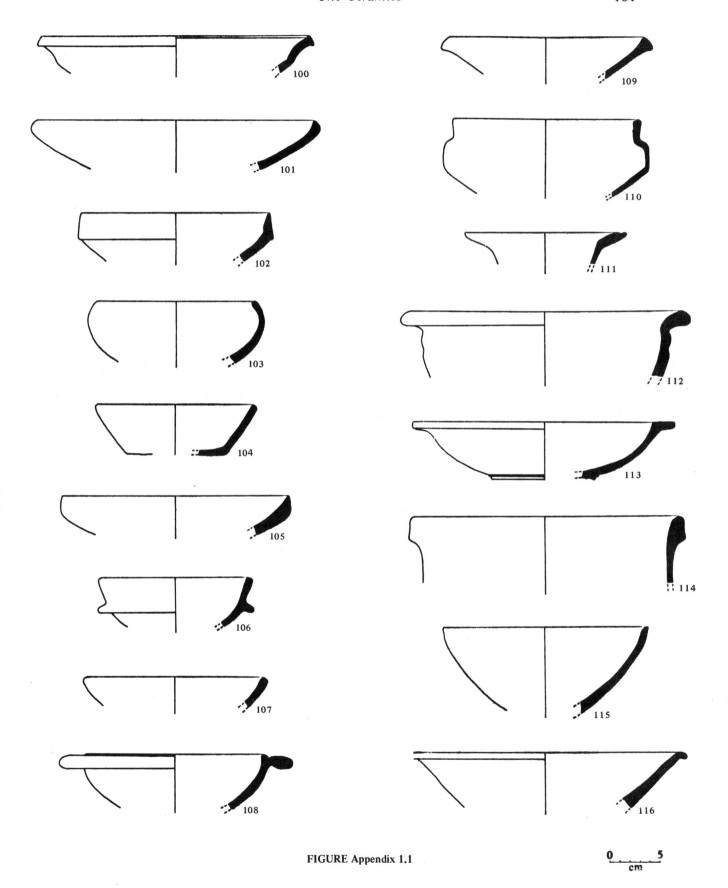

FIGURE Appendix 1.1

0   5
cm

TYPE	MUNSELL COLOR CHART READING	DESCRIPTION
117	10R 5/8	fine sand/grit temper, very little vegetable temper, some limestone inclusions; medium to high fired.
118	5R 5/6	fine sand temper, some vegetable temper; black core with exterior slip or burnishing (?); medium fired; occasionally with horizontal handle.
119	10R 5/6	large grit temper, medium vegetable temper; black core, traces of white slip on interior; medium to low fired.
120	10YR 5/8	grit temper, some vegetable temper; even color throughout with exterior red slip; medium to high fired.
121	2.5YR 4/6	grit temper, little vegetable temper; lighter color core; high fired.
122	2.5Y 6/2	sand temper, no vegetable temper; pink core; high fired.
123	10YR 7/2.5	fine sand/grit temper, no vegetable temper; white slip on exterior; medium fired.
124	5YR 4/6	coarse grit temper, some limestone inclusions; greyish core; medium fired.
125	5YR 6/3	grit temper, much vegetable temper; grey/black core; low to medium fired.
126	10R 5/6	sand temper, some vegetable temper, some limestone inclusions; black/grey core, reddish slip on exterior and interior; high fired.
127	7.5YR 8/6	fine grit temper, no vegetable temper; even color; medium fired.
128		type 128 is miscellaneous blue glazes.
129	5YR 6/6	sand/grit temper, some vegetable temper; even color throughout; medium fired.
130	5YR 5/6	chaff/grit temper; dark grey core; medium fired; along exterior rim are small pre-firing thumb impressions.
131	2.5YR 8/4	grit temper, vegetable temper, limestone inclusions; yellow/white slip over pink core; medium fired.
132	7.5YR 7/4	very coarse grit temper, heavy vegetable temper; grey to black core; medium to high fired; white slip (7.5YR 7/4) with frequent crude red/plum decoration (2YR 5/6).
133	5YR 4.5/7	very coarse grit/sand temper, moderate vegetable temper; grey to plum core; low fired.

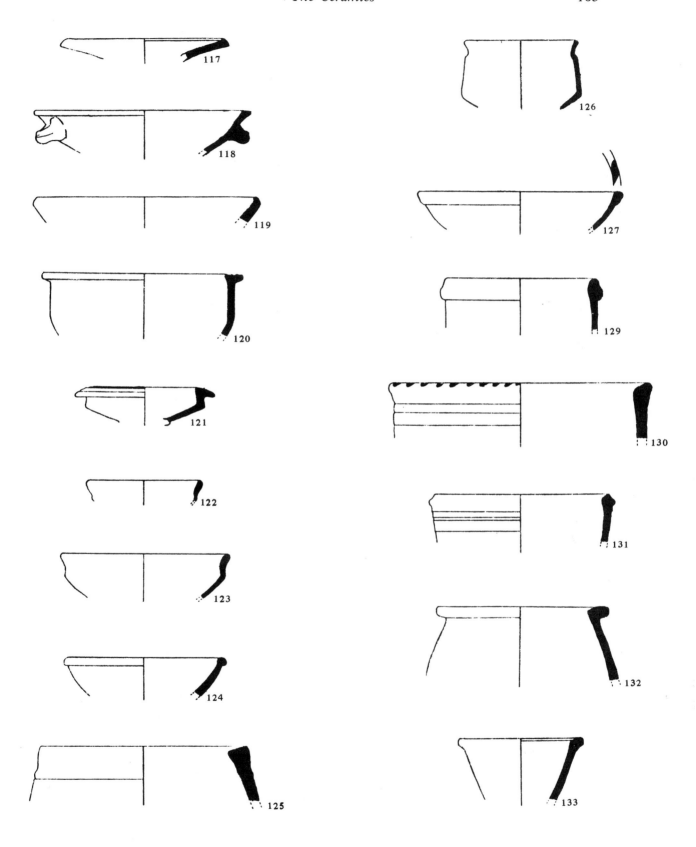

FIGURE Appendix 1.2

0   5
cm

TYPE	MUNSELL COLOR CHART READING	DESCRIPTION
134	2.5YR 5/6	sand/grit temper, vegetable temper, limestone inclusions, black/grey core; medium fired.
135	7.5YR 6/4	coarse grit temper, heavy vegetable temper; black core; medium fired; could be large jar rim or pot stand.
136	2.5YR 4/8	sand temper, heavy vegetable temper, limestone inclusions; core black except for 5 mm periphery, which is bright orange on both exterior and interior; medium fired; bottom surface extremely rough.
137	2.5YR 5/6	coarse grit temper, heavy vegetable temper; black core; medium fired.
138	10R 5/6	grit and vegetable temper; grey core; medium fired; pre-firing cord-impressions on exterior.
139	2.5YR 5/4	sand/grit temper, vegetable temper, some limestone inclusions; pinkish core; medium fired.
140	7.5YR 7/4	fine sand temper, little vegetable temper, a few limestone inclusions; even color throughout; medium fired.
141	2.5YR 6/4	sand temper, little vegetable temper, with limestone flakes; darker core; medium to high fired.
142	10R 4.5/4	sand temper, vegetable temper, limestone inclusions; medium to high fired.
143	5YR 5/3	sand/grit temper, much vegetable temper; orange core; medium to high fired.
144	10R 4/6	sand/grit temper, heavy chaff temper; black core; low fired.
145	2.5Y 7/2	fine sand temper, no vegetable temper; even color throughout; high fired.
146	5YR 4/6	sand temper, some vegetable temper; darker core; medium fired; black slip (bitumen?) on interior.
147	2.5YR 5/4	sand/grit temper, some vegetable temper; even color throughout; medium fired.
148	2.5YR 4/6	grit and vegetable temper; black core, with white slip (5YR 7.5/2) over orange (2.5YR 4/6); low fired.
149	5YR 7/4	sand/grit temper, some vegetable temper.
150	2.5Y 7/4	sand and vegetable temper; buff core; high fired.

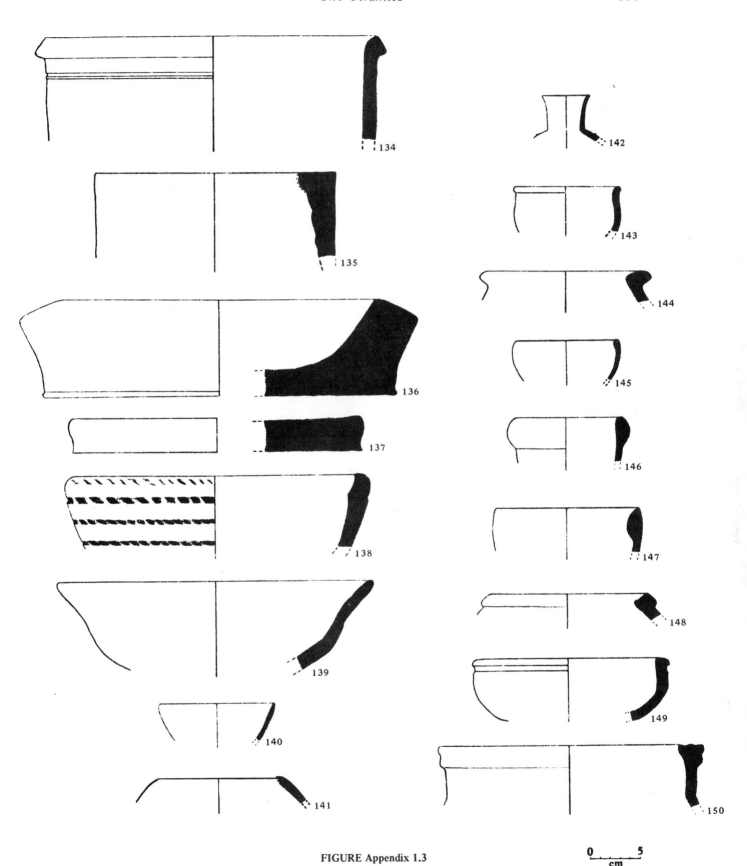

FIGURE Appendix 1.3

TYPE	MUNSELL COLOR CHART READING	DESCRIPTION
200	2.5Y 7/2	sand/grit temper, some vegetable temper; even color throughout; high fired.
201	2.5YR 5/6	coarse grit temper, some vegetable temper, some limestone inclusions; medium to high fired; folded-over rim.
202	2.5YR 5/6	fine grit temper, little vegetable temper; black core; medium fired.
203	2.5YR 4/6	medium grit temper, some vegetable temper; black core; high fired.
204	10R 4/8	sand/grit temper, some vegetable temper; black core, with light yellow paint on exterior; medium to high fired.
205	2.5YR 4/6	coarse, black grit temper, no vegetable temper; grey core; high fired.
206	7.5YR 5/4	coarse grit temper, medium vegetable temper, some limestone inclusions; black/grey core; medium to high fired.
207	5YR 4/6	fine grit temper, little vegetable temper; orange interior; medium fired.
208	2.5YR 5/6	grit temper, with many small black grit particles; medium fired.
209	2.5YR 5/8	medium coarse sand temper, many limestone inclusions; even color throughout; medium to high fired.
210	2.5Y 7/2	grit temper, little vegetable temper, limestone inclusions; grey core; medium to high fired.
211	5YR 4/8	medium grit temper, very little vegetable temper; black core, exterior slip (7.5YR 8/4); medium fired.
212	2.5YR 6/6	coarse grit temper, heavy vegetable temper; black core, with traces of white slip or wash; medium to low fired.
213	2.5Y 7/4	vegetable and sand temper; even color throughout; high fired.
214	10YR 8/3	sand/grit temper; orange interior; high fired.
215	10YR 5.5/3	sand temper, little vegetable temper, with small limestone inclusions; even color throughout; very high fired.
216	10R 5/6	sand/grit temper, heavy chaff temper, limestone inclusions; pinkish core; medium fired.

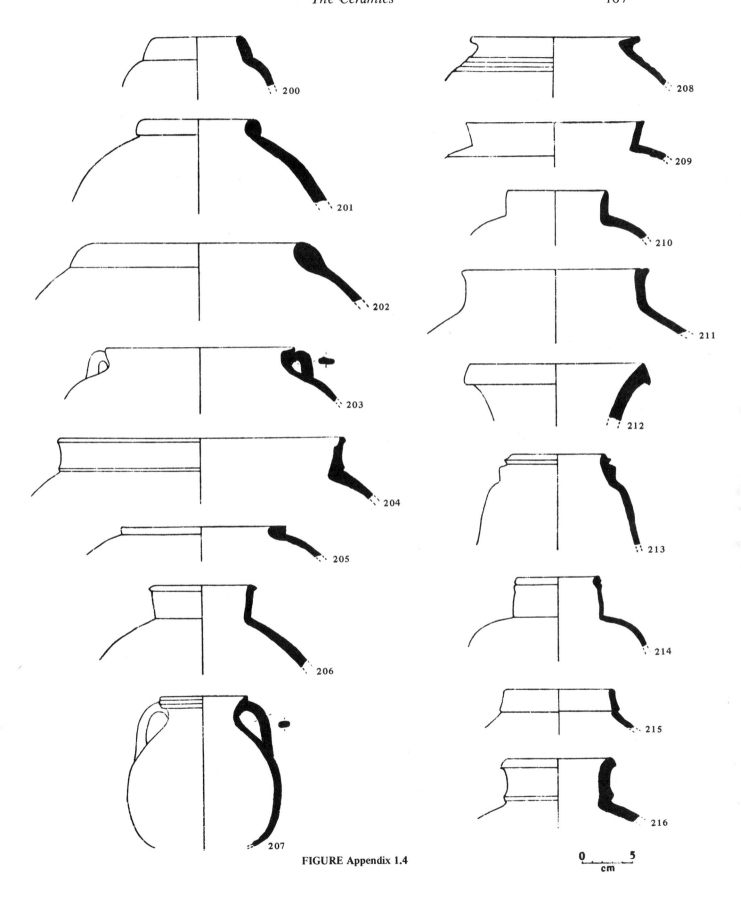

FIGURE Appendix 1.4

TYPE	MUNSELL COLOR CHART READING	DESCRIPTION
217	10R 5/6	fine sand temper, some vegetable temper; black core, red slip; high fired.
218	10R 4/8	fine sand temper, some vegetable temper, some limestone inclusions; even color throughout; medium to high fired.
219	10R 3/6	grit temper, some vegetable temper; black core, with red slip; high fired.
220	2.5YR 4/6	chaff temper, limestone inclusions; black/grey core; medium to high fired.
221	5YR 7/6	fine sand temper; plum colored core, orange interior; high fired.
222	10R 5/6	sand temper, heavy chaff temper, some limestone inclusions; black core; medium to high fired.
223	2.5YR 4/6	grit temper, very heavy vegetable temper; pink/grey core; high fired.
224	10YR 8/4	heavy vegetable temper; grey core, with yellow slip (10YR 8/4) and red decoration (2.5YR 4/4); medium to high fired.
225	5YR 5/5	grit temper, no vegetable temper; even color; medium fired.
226	10YR 4/2	grit temper, little vegetable temper; "smoked" exterior (10YR 4/2) over even core and interior (5YR 5/4); medium to high fired.
227	2.5YR 6/6	vegetable and grit temper, with limestone flakes; even color; medium fired.
228	5YR 6/6	vegetable and sand temper, limestone inclusions; even color; high fired.
229	5YR 6/6	grit temper, heavy vegetable temper, many limestone inclusions and flakes; dark grey core, wheel-marked interior; medium fired.
230	2.5YR 5/6	sand/grit temper, vegetable temper, limestone inclusions; high fired.

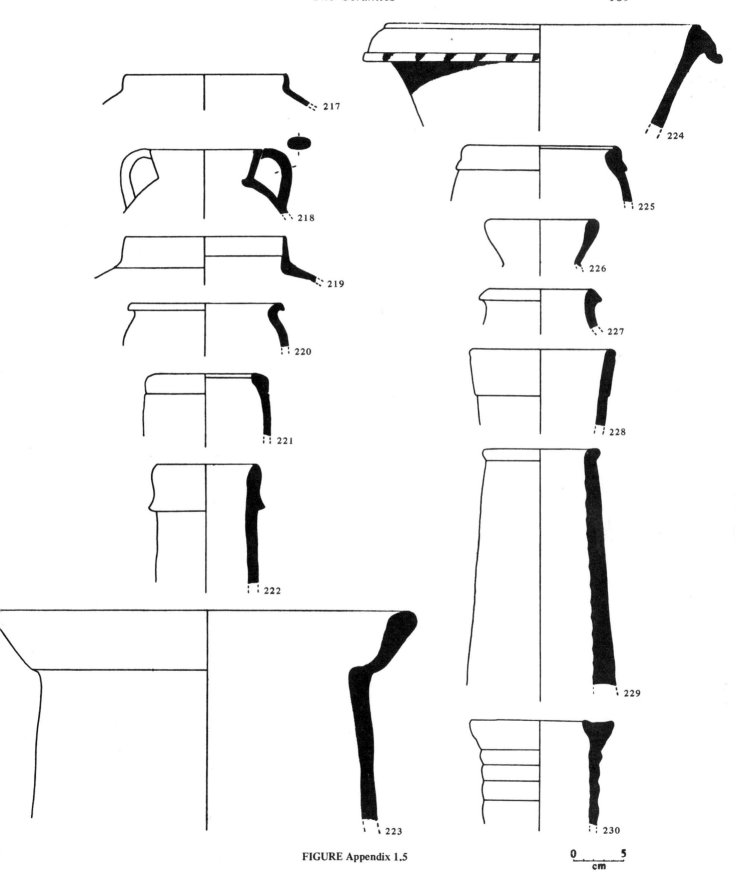

FIGURE Appendix 1.5

0   5
cm

TYPE	MUNSELL COLOR CHART READING	DESCRIPTION
231	2.5Y 8/4	grit temper, heavy vegetable temper, limestone inclusions; grey core, with yellow slip (2.5Y 8/4) over orange body (2.5YR 5/4); medium fired.
232	5YR 7/6	grit temper, vegetable temper, with limestone flakes; medium fired.
233	2.5YR 5/6	grit temper, little vegetable temper; even color; medium to high fired.
234	2.5YR 5/4	grit temper, heavy vegetable temper, grey core; high fired.
235	5YR 3/4	grit/sand temper, medium vegetable temper; black core; medium to high fired.
236	5YR 5/6	sand temper, heavy vegetable temper, with limestone flakes; pink core, with white plaster on rim and exterior; medium to high fired.
237	2.5YR 3/6	grit temper, heavy vegetable temper; black core; high fired.
238	5YR 6/6	vegetable/grit temper, with some limestone flakes; pink core; medium fired.
239	5YR 5/4	vegetable/grit temper; even color; medium to high fired.
240		miscellaneous glazed jar rims.
241	10R 3/4	sand temper, little vegetable temper; pink core; high fired.
242	5YR 6/4	grit temper, heavy vegetable temper; even color; low to medium fired.
243	2.5YR 4/4	sand/grit temper, vegetable temper; grey core; medium to high fired.
244	2.5YR 5/6	sand/grit temper, some vegetable temper; grey core, with exterior and interior red slip; high fired.
245	2.5YR 4/6	sand temper, heavy vegetable temper; grey core; high fired.

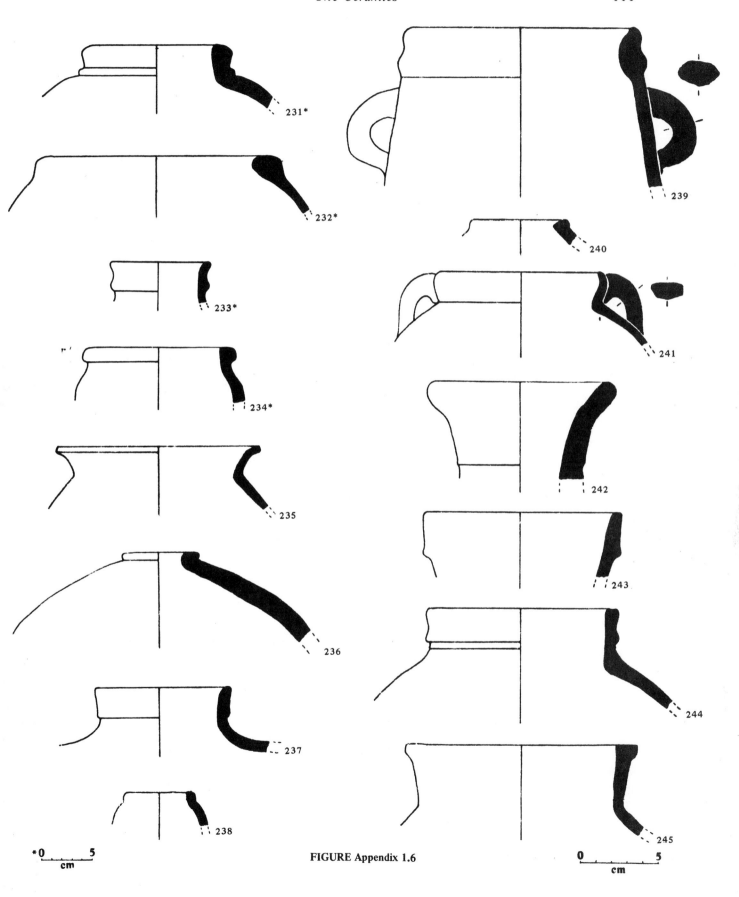

FIGURE Appendix 1.6

TYPE	MUNSELL COLOR CHART READING	DESCRIPTION
300	7.5YR 7/4	vegetable/sand temper; even color; medium to high fired.
301	5YR 5/4	grit temper, some vegetable temper; even color; medium fired.
302	2.5YR 4/6	sand temper, no vegetable temper; black core, with exterior and interior burnishing; very high fired.
303	2.5YR 4/4	grit temper, no vegetable temper; even color; medium to high fired.
304	2.5YR 4/6	vegetable/grit temper; even color, with interior and exterior red slip; medium fired.
305	5YR 3/4	grit temper, no vegetable temper; grey core; high fired.
306	10R 4/8	fine sand temper, no vegetable temper; exterior burnished ("Roman"); very high fired.
307	5YR 5/6	grit temper, heavy vegetable temper; grey/black core; medium fired.
308	2.5YR 4/4	sand temper, no vegetable temper; lighter colored core, interior red-slipped; high fired.
309	2.5YR 5/6	vegetable/grit temper, with limestone flakes; even color; medium to high fired.
310	2.5YR 5/6	sand/grit temper, vegetable temper, limestone inclusions; lighter pink core; low fired.
311	2.5YR 4/8	vegetable/grit temper; black core; medium fired; string-cut base.
312	10YR 4/2	vegetable/grit temper; even color; medium to high fired; string-cut base.
313	5YR 6/4	vegetable/sand temper; even color; medium fired; string-cut base.
314	5YR 6/6	grit temper, heavy vegetable temper; greyish core; medium fired; type number is for base only.
315	5YR 5/4	vegetable/sand temper; black core; medium fired.
316	7.5YR N2	sand temper, little vegetable temper; lighter grey core; high fired; interior stamped design.
317	2.5YR 4/6	sand temper, no vegetable temper; light orange core, with darker orange slip on exterior and interior; medium fired.

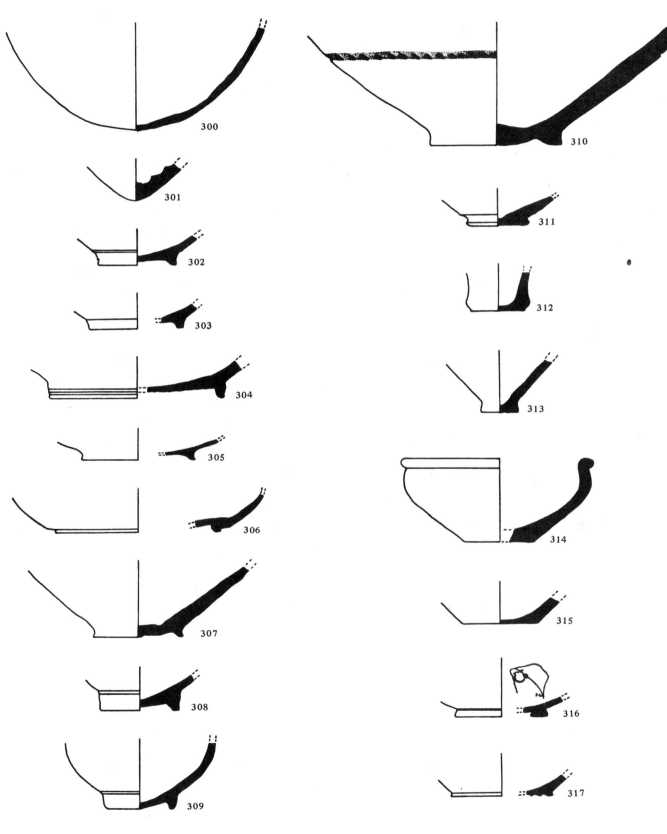

0   5
cm

TYPE	MUNSELL COLOR CHART READING	DESCRIPTION
318	2.5YR 5/6	vegetable/grit temper; even color; medium fired.
319	2.5YR 5.5/4	sand temper, some vegetable temper; even color, with interior pinkish slip; high fired.
320	5YR 4/4	vegetable/grit temper; even color; medium fired.
321	2.5YR 5/6	grit temper, heavy vegetable temper; grey core; medium fired.
322	2.5YR 4/6	grit temper, heavy chaff temper; black core; high fired.
323	10YR 8/4	sand/vegetable temper, large limestone inclusions; buff core, pinkish interior; medium to high fired.
324	5YR 7/4	fine sand temper, no vegetable temper, large limestone inclusions; even color; high fired.
325	5YR 7/6	vegetable/grit temper, with limestone flakes; even color; very high fired.
326	10YR 8/4	vegetable/fine sand temper; even color; medium to high fired.
327	5YR 6/6	sand/grit temper, some vegetable temper; even color; medium fired.
328	5YR 5/6	vegetable/grit temper; even color throughout, many examples have bitumen-coated interiors; low to medium fired.
329	5YR 6/6	fine sand/grit temper, very little vegetable temper; medium fired.

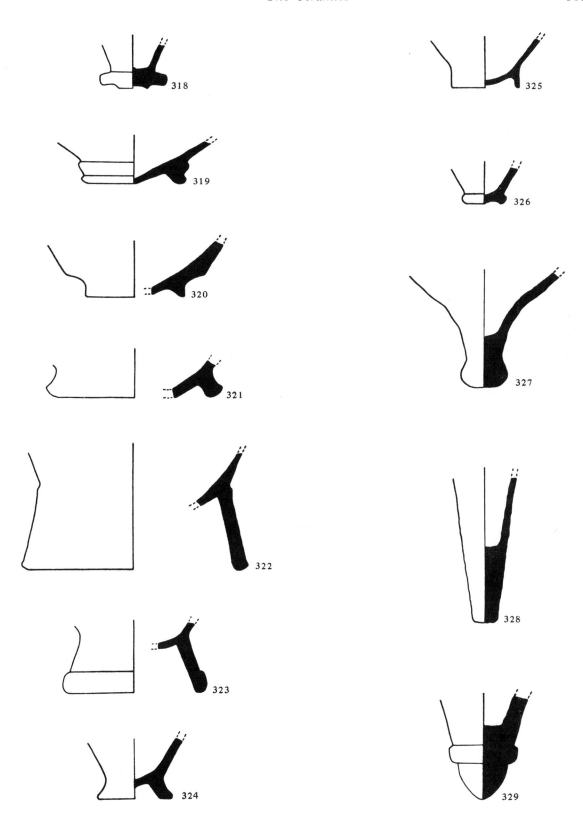

FIGURE Appendix 1.8

TYPE	MUNSELL COLOR CHART READING	DESCRIPTION
330	10YR 7/4	fine sand temper, some vegetable temper; even color; very high fired.
331	10YR 7/3	grit temper, vegetable temper; even color; medium fired; on the interior of this base is a piece of clay (pre-firing infixed) with holes.
332	5YR 7/2	chaff/sand temper; even color, with interior and exterior pale slip; medium fired.
333	10YR 7/3	fine sand temper, no vegetable temper; orange (2.5YR 5/6) interior and core, with buff (10YR 7/3) exterior; high fired.
334	2.5YR 4/4	fine sand temper, no vegetable temper; even color; extremely high fired.
335	7.5YR 5/6	sand/grit temper, little vegetable temper; buff core; medium to high fired.
336	5YR 5/4	fine sand temper, no vegetable temper; even color; medium to high fired.
337	2.5YR 5/6	sand/grit temper, some vegetable temper; even color, with burnished interior; medium fired.
338		grit temper, little vegetable temper; blue glaze over whitish core.
339	2.5Y 8/4	sand temper, heavy vegetable temper; black core with yellow (2.5Y 8/4) slip over red (2.5YR 4/4) exterior; high fired.
340	2.5YR 5/6	grit temper, heavy vegetable temper; black core; medium fired.
341	10R 4/6	sand temper, no vegetable temper; red slip; high fired.
342	5YR 5/6	sand temper, little vegetable temper; orange core, with reddish-orange exterior; medium fired.
343	5YR 6/4	sand/grit temper, no vegetable temper; string-cut base; medium fired; type number is for base only.
344	7.5YR 6/4	sand temper, no vegetable temper; even color; high fired.

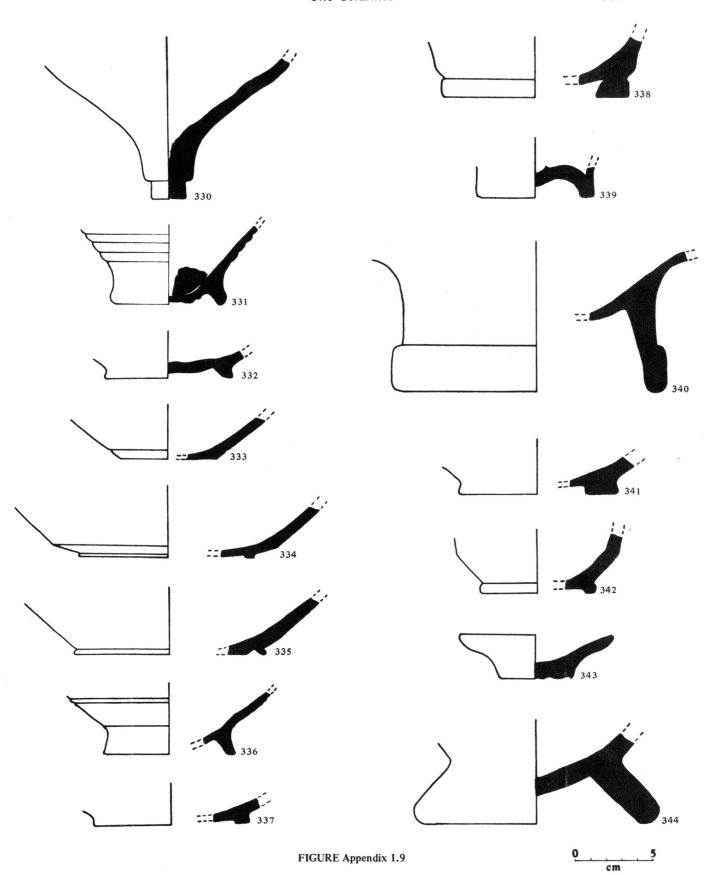

FIGURE Appendix 1.9

0   5
cm

TYPE	MUNSELL COLOR CHART READING	DESCRIPTION
500	10R 4/6	a general type number for red (10R 4/6) bowls with darker red (10R 3/2) designs.
501	2.5YR 4/4	grit temper, heavy vegetable temper; black/grey core; high fired.
508	2.5Y 8/4	sand temper, little vegetable temper; grey core, with brown paint on interior; very high fired.
512	2.5YR 5/4	sand temper, no vegetable temper; grey core; high fired.
515		dark blue glazed bowl, with vegetable/grit temper.
516		transparent glass base.
517		deep purple glass base.
518		transparent glass rim.
519		brownish-purple glass bowl.
520		light to medium green glass bowl.
522	5YR 5/4	grit temper, heavy vegetable temper; black core; medium fired; lug handle (?).
524		alabaster bowl.
525	7.5YR 4/2	heavy grit temper, some vegetable temper, limestone inclusions; grey core; medium fired; body sherd with spout.
529	2.5YR 4/6	grit temper, heavy vegetable temper; grey core; high fired.
530		dark blue glazed bowl.
531		limestone bowl.

FIGURE Appendix 1.10

POTTERY TYPES NOT ILLUSTRATED

TYPE	MUNSELL COLOR CHART READING	DESCRIPTION
400		a general type number for medium to large handles with sand/grit temper and a "spine" down the back.
401	2.5YR 5/6	small, vertical handle on jar rim, with vegetable/sand temper.
402		large, high fired, sand tempered handles, buff to orange in color.
403		miscellaneous small handles.
404		miscellaneous medium handles.
405		miscellaneous large handles.
406		large, heavy vegetable tempered brown/red handle with black core.
407		large lug handle, with heavy vegetable temper, black core, and red exterior.
408		medium lug handle, high-fired, with heavy vegetable temper, grey core, and buff slip over red exterior.
409		small to medium grit-tempered handle, orange exterior with grey core.
410		small sand/vegetable-tempered handle.
411		large, crudely-made, vegetable-tempered, buff-colored handles.
412		small to medium, vegetable-tempered, buff-colored handles.
413		buff-colored, sand/grit tempered handle; in cross-section like two joined circles.
414		small to medium, grit-tempered, buff-colored vertical handles.
415		medium handle with some vegetable temper, sand/grit temper, and a grey/black core with red/brown exterior.

TYPE	MUNSELL COLOR CHART READING	DESCRIPTION
502	5YR 5/4	body sherds: vegetable/grit temper, with small pebble inclusions; even colored core, red exterior with buff paint in circular design; medium fired.
503		red/brown body sherds with dark paint.
504	2.5Y 8/4	body sherds: sand temper, little vegetable temper; buff with red paint on exterior; medium fired.
505	2.5YR 3/6	body sherds: vegetable/grit temper; grey core; with buff paint on exterior.
506	2.5YR 5/4	body sherds: vegetable/grit temper; grey core and interior; mottled buff paint on exterior.
507	7.5YR 5/4	body sherds: sand temper, heavy vegetable temper; black core, then red, then buff exterior with red paint; medium to high fired.
509	10YR 7/4	sand-/vegetable-tempered, buff-colored (10YR 7/4) body sherds with dark (7.5YR 3/2) paint.
510		body sherds with pseudo-rope impressions.
511	5YR 6/6	body sherds: grit temper, heavy vegetable temper; with exterior (pre-firing) incised designs.
513	2.5YR 4/4	body sherds: sand temper, no vegetable temper; high fired; with interior circular incised design.
514		blue glazed body sherds.
523	10YR 4/2	vegetable-/sand-tempered, mold-made oil lamp fragments (?).
526	2.5YR 4/6	painted animal figure: vegetable temper; black core, with red exterior and buff, red, and black paint; medium to high fired.
527	10YR 7/6	mold-made, broken oil lamp fragments (?).
528		animal head figure; vegetable temper, sand temper; red exterior with buff, red, and brown painted designs.
532		green glazed body sherds.

APPENDIX II: NUMISMATIC EVIDENCE

ROBERT J. WENKE

University of Washington, Seattle

Only three partially identifiable coins were found during the 1980 season, two from the surface of el-Hibeh's northern precincts, the other from disturbed, secondary deposits in Level 1 of TS1a.

All three coins, which now are in the Egyptian Museum's collections, were so badly eroded that no pictures or drawings would prove illuminating. Dr. N. D. Nicol, formerly Acting Director of the Cairo Office of the Library of Congress, kindly examined these coins for us, and we are grateful to him for his assistance.

In his opinion, all three coins are probably bronze issues of the first few centuries A.D. The coin excavated from Level 1 of TS1a is about 13 mm in diameter and may bear the name "Arcadius," a Roman emperor of the late fourth and early fifth century A.D. The reverse of this coin was badly eroded. The two coins found on the surface were 22 mm and 11 mm in diameter, respectively. Dr. Nicol suggested the larger coin may be an Alexandrine issue of the mid-third century A.D. and the smaller one of late Byzantine or early Islamic date, but these possible assignments are based mainly on size and shape—there are few surface details evident.

A large number of well-preserved coins was recovered from el-Hibeh by the Italian mission of the early 1930s (Paribeni 1935). The earliest of these coins dates to Ptolemy III, who reigned from 246 to 221 B.C., and the last to Constantius II, who reigned from A.D. 337 to 361. The great majority of the more than twenty-five coins recovered belong to the reign of Nero and date to between A.D. 45 and 68. The most frequent issues of the second century A.D. are of Probus (c. A.D. 276-282), and from the third century A.D. the most common coins found at el-Hibeh are issues of Lucinius and Constantine the Great.

APPENDIX III: EPIGRAPHIC MATERIALS

ROBERT J. WENKE
University of Washington, Seattle

One aspect of the el-Hibeh project was a systematic restudy of the 22nd Dynasty temple at the site. The inscriptions and architecture of this structure were described by Ranke (1926), and our objective in 1980 was to confirm and extend, if possible, his analysis.

The results of this work will be published at a later date by Cynthia May Sheikholeslami.

The only other epigraphic materials recovered during the 1980 season were stamped bricks, some papyri fragments, one inscribed pot sherd, and an inscribed lamp base. These are illustrated in Plates 1 and 2 for this Appendix.

Laboratory photographs of these objects are in the possession of Cynthia Sheikholeslami (the objects, themselves, are in the Egyptian Museum), and it is anticipated that she will publish at a later date a full description, translation, and analysis of these materials. For this reason, these objects are presented here without complete information and discussion.

APPENDIX IV: SMALL FINDS

ROBERT J. WENKE

University of Washington, Seattle

Some of the small finds recovered during the 1980 season are presented in Plates 1 and 2 for this Appendix. Most of these are types of artifacts commonly found at Egyptian sites of the Late Dynastic and Ptolemaic Periods, and none is of exceptional importance.

Of some interest are the sharpened bone pieces in Plate 2. In January of 1983 the Egyptian Museum displayed arrows from Old Kingdom tombs at Saqqara that were tipped with bone elements extremely similar to those found at el-Hibeh, even to the faint red discoloration on some of the tips. This red color is described by museum officials as the residue of a poison. There is no reason not to believe that the el-Hibeh finds were used as projectile points. But these objects also resemble objects used in weaving. They are quite unlike, however, bone implements used in the application of cosmetics.

Many beads and faience amulet fragments were found that are not illustrated here. Comparisons with materials from other sites indicate that none of these is unique. All amulet fragments with discernible signs are presented in Plate 1.

Not illustrated in detail is the diversity of wood items found at el-Hibeh. Although no wooden combs were found in TS1 or TS2, these artifacts litter the site's surface, and they seem in shape indistinguishable from those found at comparable sites (Bresciani 1968, 1976). Other wooden objects are presently undergoing analysis to identify the species of trees from which they were made.

It is anticipated that a more complete record and analysis of the small finds from el-Hibeh will be published in an additional report.

APPENDIX V: THE REGIONAL SURVEY

ROBERT J. WENKE

University of Washington, Seattle

The resources and the limits of our research permit were such that we could not undertake a systematic site survey in areas adjacent to el-Hibeh. But it was possible to examine on foot the area extending about 10 km east of the site, and this revealed a few occupations of interest.

The first of these was the massive concentration of looted graves that extends over at least .75 km² and is located approximately 5 km east of el-Hibeh—although lack of aerial photographs made the exact location of these graves with reference to el-Hibeh difficult to determine. The existence of this necropolis has long been known, although it has never been systematically studied. Burials of every period of el-Hibeh's occupation are probably represented in this cemetery, but without systematic collections it would be difficult to define the period of maximum use. There were virtually no visible sarcophagi fragments of the type that occur by the score in the desert a few hundred meters east of el-Hibeh, nor were certain kinds of Roman pottery, such as the early *Arretine*-style wares, Eastern Sigillata wares, and Late Roman B and C fabrics (Hayes 1972; Breccia 1934, Whitcomb and Johnson 1979, fig. C4c-4) evident on superficial examination. Surprisingly little pottery was on the surface of most areas, but there were many fragments of wood coffins. The necropolis is so thoroughly looted that little of scientific interest is likely to remain.

Epigraphic reports from the area of el-Hibeh are sufficiently unspecific as to what areas were being looted for papyri that it cannot be established with certainty that any of the many Greek papyri thought to have originated from el-Hibeh were actually found in this cemetery area (Kamal 1901; Botti 1945, 1955; Grenfell and Hunt 1906-1955). Kamal excavated for seven days in this area, but his report is of little use, since he specifies nothing about the location, depth, or method of his work (1901:90-91).

Generally, there is nothing in his description of his finds that is not consistent with a late New Kingdom and Late Period provenience. On the basis of the fleeting examination of the ceramics on this part of the necropolis, I would suggest that it was also in use in the Ptolemaic period.

Other sites of interest to the east of el-Hibeh include several concentrations of worked flints along the Pleistocene Nile banks. None of these concentrations was sufficiently dense as to suggest sustained occupation, and the only unambiguous tools found were two retouched blades of the type usually assigned to "Late Paleolithic" (parallels in Whitcomb and Johnson 1979:283, fig. 38). There should be many tools and sites along the banks of the Nile's Pleistocene course, but although we were able to identify the formations likely to be remnants of Pleistocene Nile beaches and wadis, one full day's survey turned up only a few artifacts—perhaps because the preponderance of naturally occurring flints masked the archaeological sites. Also, some such sites may have been buried beneath river gravels and wadi deposits during the more moist intervals and high Nile floods.

The only ancient settlement discovered during the survey and not (so far as I know) previously reported is at the foot of the 60 meter terrace about 10 km east of el-Hibeh. An "L" shaped mudbrick wall encloses the site, the northeastern edge of which is bounded by the limestone scarp that rises steeply on this edge of the settlement. The apparent lack of architecture inside the walls and the low density of pottery and other artifacts argue a short term, perhaps specialized, occupation. The site is near what are listed on maps of this area as camel tracks into the interior toward the Red Sea, and thus the site may have been a way-station on this route. Only a cursory examination of the pottery was possible, and it seemed that most of the ceramics were of types present on the non-Roman areas of el-Hibeh, and thus may be of Late Period date.

Future work at el-Hibeh should include test excavations and surface collections at this site, because these would provide a ceramic assemblage of short interval and possibly economically specific range, thereby aiding in sorting out el-Hibeh's ceramic chronology and functional assemblages.

Additional surveys should also be undertaken along Pleistocene wadis and banks to the east of el-Hibeh, for it is likely that this was a rich environment for Pleistocene hunting and collecting societies.

APPENDIX VI: REPORT ON THE PETROLOGY
OF THE TEMPLE AT EL-HIBEH

M. HASSAAN EL-HASSAANY and TAREK NAFFIE
al-Azhar University, Cairo

The 22nd Dynasty temple at el-Hibeh was built of limestone blocks, probably quarried from the limestone scarp near the site. These limestone formations occur in at least five different layers of Middle Eocene age and are of different hardnesses. Thin section studies under a polarizing microscope of five samples from these blocks (found as fragments at the base of the temple walls) revealed that the temple was built of blocks taken from at least two different layers of limestone. One of the samples had a faunal content quite different from that of the others, and may have been part of a block brought from elsewhere in the Nile Valley. The markedly different state of preservation of various blocks in the temple's walls probably reflects the different hardnesses of the various layers of limestone from which the blocks were quarried.

Several pieces of granite and one fragment of sandstone were found near and in the temple, and these have been subjected to a complete microscopic examination (by Tarek Naffie). The granite fragments are almost certainly from Aswan, whereas the sandstone is of the type characteristic of Nubia. None of these fragments showed obvious signs of sculpting, although they were so small that they may well have been (at least in the case of the granite) fragments of sculptures or temple decoration.

BIBLIOGRAPHY

ADAMS, R. McC.
> 1965   *Land Behind Baghdad: A History of Settlement on the Diyala Plains.* Chicago: University of Chicago Press.
> 1966   *The Evolution of Urban Society.* Chicago: Aldine.
> 1972   Patterns of urbanization in early Southern Mesopotamia. In P. Ucko, et al., eds., *Man, Settlement, and Urbanism.* London: Duckworth.
> 1981   *Heartland of Cities.* Chicago: University of Chicago Press.

AMERICAN ASSOCIATION OF TEXTILE CHEMISTS AND COLORISTS
> 1979   *AATCC Technical Manual,* Vol. 55. Triangle Park.

AMUS, P., and R. SA'AD
> 1971   Habitations de prêtres dans le temple d'Amon á Karnak. *Kemi* 21:217-238.

ANTHES, R.
> 1955   *Mit Rahineh.* Philadelphia: University of Pennsylvania Press.

BAER, K.
> 1973   The Libyan and Nubian kings of Egypt: Notes on the chronology of Dynasties XXII-XXVI. *Journal of Near Eastern Studies* 32:4-25.

BECKERATH, J. VON
> 1966   The Nile level records at Karnak and their importance for the history of the Libyan period. *Journal of the American Research Center in Egypt* 5:43-55.

BELLINGER, LOUISE
> 1950   *Textile Analysis: Early Techniques in Egypt and the Near East.* Textile Museum Workshop Notes. Paper 2. Washington, D.C.: The Textile Museum.
> 1951   *Textile Analysis: Early Techniques in Egypt and the Near East, Part 2.* Textile Museum Workshop Notes. Paper 3. Washington, D.C.: The Textile Museum.

BENFER, R.
> 1975   Sampling and Classification. In J. Mueller, ed., *Sampling in Archaeology.* Tucson: University of Arizona Press.

BERGMAN, INGRID
> 1975   *Late Nubian Textiles, Scandinavian Joint Expedition to Sudanese Nubia.* Vol. 8. Lund.

BIERBRIER, M. L.
> 1975   *The Late New Kingdom in Egypt (c. 1300-664 B.C.).* Warminster: Aris & Phillips.

BIETAK, M.
  1979   Urban archaeology and the "town problem" in Ancient Egypt. In K. Weeks, ed., *Egyptology and the Social Sciences*. Cairo: The American University in Cairo Press.

BINFORD, L. and S. BINFORD
  1966   A preliminary analysis of functional variability in the Mousterian of Levallois Facies. *American Anthropologist* (special publication) 68(2)2:238-95.

BOESSNECK, J.
  1976   Tell El-Dab'a. *Oster. Akad. Wissen., Denk. Gesam.*, V.

BOSERUP, E.
  1965   *The Conditions of Agricultural Growth*. Chicago: Aldine.

BOTHMER, B., et al.
  1963   *Egyptian Sculpture of the Late Period*. Brooklyn: The Brooklyn Museum.

BOTTI, G.
  1945   Alcuni tipi di sarcofagi e casse di mummie provenienti degli scavi fiorentini di el Hibeh. In *Scritti dedicati alla memoria di Ippoliti Rosellini ecc.* 1945:85-108, pl. 12-18.
  1955   Le monete alessandrini da El Hibeh nel Museo Egizio di Firenze. *Aegyptus* 35:245-274, pl. 1-12.
  1958   Le casse di mummie e i sarcofagi da El Hibeh nel Museo Egizio di Firenze. *Accademia Toscana di Scienze e Lettere* "La Columbaria," Studi, V.

BOURRIAU, J.
  1981   *Umm el-Ga'ab: Pottery from the Nile Valley before the Arab conquest*. Catalogue of the Exhibition organized by the Fitzwilliam Museum. Cambridge: Cambridge University Press.

BRANDFORD, JOANNE SEGAL
  1977   The Semna South Textiles. ms.

BRECCIA, E.
  1934   *Terracotta figurati grecchiegreco-eglizi del Museo Alessandria*. Bergamo.

BRESCIANI, E.
  1968   *Rapporto Preliminare Delle Campagne Di Scavo 1966 e 1967*. Milan: Istituto Editoriale Cisalpino.
  1976   *Rapporto Preliminare Delle Campagne Di Scavo 1968 e 1969*. Milan: Istituto Editoriale Cisalpino.

BROOKNER, JONATHAN
  1979   Textiles. In D. S. Whitcomb and J. H. Johnson, eds., *Quseir al-Qadim 1978: Preliminary Report*, Chapter 5. Cairo: American Research Center in Egypt, Inc.

BROOKS, C.
  1949   *Climate through the Ages*. New York: McGraw-Hill.

BROUK, B.
    1975   *Plants Consumed by Man.* London: Academic Press.

BROWN, T. W. and M. BOHGOT
    1938   Date Palm in Egypt. *Ministry of Agriculture, Egypt, Booklet No. 24.*

BRUNTON, GUY and GERTRUDE CATON-THOMPSON
    1928   *The Badarian Civilisation and Prehistoric Remains near Badari.* London: Quaritch.

BURNHAM, DOROTHY
    1980   *Warp and Weft: A Textile Terminology.* Toronto: Royal Ontario Museum.

BURNHAM, MARK
    1975   Cleaning of Archaeological Textiles. In P. Fiske, ed., *Irene Emery Roundtable on Museum Textiles, 1974 Proceedings*, pp. 47-51. Washington, D.C.: The Textile Museum.

BUTZER, K.
    1976   *Early Hydraulic Civilization in Egypt.* Chicago: University of Chicago Press.
    1982   *Archaeology as Human Ecology.* Cambridge: Cambridge University Press.

CAMINOS, R.
    1958   The Chronicle of Prince Osorkon. *Analecta Orientalia* 37.

CATON-THOMPSON, G. and E. W. GARDNER
    1934   *The Desert Fayum.* London: Royal Anthropological Institute of Great Britain.

CAVALLI-SFORZA, L. L. and M. W. FELDMAN
    1981   *Cultural Transmission and Evolution: A Quantitative Approach.* Princeton: Princeton University Press.

CHURCHER, C. S.
    1972   Late Pleistocene Vertebrates from Archaeological Sites in the Plain of Kom Ombo, Upper Egypt. *Roy. Ont. Mus., Life Sci. Contrib., 82*

CLOSE, A.
    1980   Stylistic Analysis of the Wadi Kubbaniya Assemblages. In *Loaves and Fishes: The Prehistory of Wadi Kubbaniya*, assembled by F. Wendorf and R. Schild. Dallas: Southern Methodist University.

COHEN, R.
    1981   Evolutionary Epistemology and Human Values. *Current Anthropology* 22(3):201-218.

COIT, J. E.
    1951   Carob or St. John's Bread. *Economic Botany* 5:82-96.

COLE, J. and C. KING
    1968   *Quantitative Geography.* London: Wiley and Sons.

COLONIAL PLANT AND ANIMAL PRODUCTS
1955   Notes: Castor Seeds From Northern Rhodesia. *Colonial Plant and Animal Products* V(2): 165-166.

COWGILL, G.
1972   Models, methods, and techniques for seriation. In David L. Clarke, ed., *Models in Archaeology*. London: Methuen & Co.
1975   On causes and consequences of ancient and modern population changes. *American Anthropologist* 77(3):505-25.

COWGILL, G., WHALLON, R. and B. OTTAWAY (compilers and organizers)
1981   Union Internacional de Ciencias Prehistoricas y Protohistoricas, Coloquio Manejo de Datos y Methodos Matematicos de Arqueologia, Mexico, D.F.

CRAWFORD, DOROTHY J.
1971   *Kerkeosiris: An Egyptian Village in the Ptolemaic Period*. Cambridge: Cambridge University Press.
1979   Food: Tradition and Change in Hellenistic Egypt. *World Archaeology* 11(2):136-146.

CROWFOOT, GRACE
1958   Textiles, Basketry and Mats. In C. Singer, et. al., eds., *A History of Technology*, Vol. 1, pp. 416-456. Oxford: Clarendon Press.

DARBY, WILLIAM, PAUL GHALIOUNGUI, and LOUIS GRIVETTI
1977   *Food the Gift of Osiris*. New York: Academic Press.

DARESSY, G.
1902   Le temple de Hibeh. *Annales du Service des Antiquités de l'Égypte* 2:154-6.
1903   Un cercueil de Hibeh. *Annales du Service des Antiquités de l'Égypte* 4:116-119.

DEETZ, J. and E. DETHLEFSEN
1965   The Doppler-effect and archaeology: A consideration of the spatial aspects of seriation. *Southwestern Journal of Anthropology* 21:196-206.

DIENER, P. and R. ROBKIN
1978   Ecology, Evolution, and the Search for Cultural Origins. *Current Anthropology* 19(3):493-540.

DORAN, J. and F. HODSON
1975   *Mathematics and Computers in Archaeology*. Cambridge (Mass.): Harvard University Press.

DOUGENIK, J. and D. SHEEHAN
1975   *SYMAP User's Reference Manual*. Cambridge (Mass.): Harvard University Press.

DRENNAN, R.
1976   A refinement of chronological seriation using nonmetric multidimensional scaling. *American Antiquity* 41(3):290-302.

DUDGEON, G. C. and G. BALLAND
    1916   Work in Connection With Egyptian Wheat. Ministry of Agriculture, Egypt, *Technical and Scientific Service Bulletin No. 7* (Botanical Section).

DUERST, J. U.
    1926   Vergleichende Untersuchungsmethoden am Skelett bei Säugern. *Abderhalden's Handbuch der Biologischen Arbeitsmethoden*, VII, Vol. 2.

DUKE, JAMES
    1981   *Handbook of Legumes of World Economic Importance.* New York: Plenum Press.

DUNNELL, R.
    1970   Seriation method and its evaluation. *American Antiquity* 35(3):305-319.
    1980   Evolutionary theory and archaeology. In M. B. Schiffer, ed., *Advances in Archaeological Method and Theory*, vol. 3, pp. 35-99. New York: Academic Press.
    1981   Seriation, groups, and measurements. Union International de Ciencias Prehistoricas y Arqueologia, Mexico, D.F.
    1982   Science, Social Science, and Common Sense: The Agonizing Dilemma of Modern Archaeology. *Journal of Anthropological Research* 38 (Spring 1982): pp. 1-24.

DUNNELL, R. and R. WENKE
    1979   An evolutionary model of the development of complex societies. Paper presented at the annual meeting of the American Association for the Advancement of Science, San Francisco, Ca.

EASTWOOD, GILLIAN
    1982   Textiles. In D. S. Whitcomb and J. H. Johnson, eds., *Quseir al-Qadim 1980: Preliminary Report*, pp. 285-326. Malibu: Undena Publications.

EISENSTADT, S.
    1967   *The Decline of Empires.* Englewood Cliffs: Prentice-Hall.

EL-HADIDI, NABIL M. and LOUTFY BOULOS
    1979   *Street Trees in Egypt.* Cairo.

EL-HADIDI, NABIL M. and JANA KOSINOVA
    1971   Studies on the Weed Flora of Cultivated Land in Egypt. 1. Preliminary Survey. *Mitteilung Botanischen Staatssammlung*. Munchen. 10:354-367.

EMERY, IRENE
    1966   *The Primary Structures of Fabrics*, Washington, D.C.: The Textile Museum.

EPSTEIN, H.
    1971   *The Origin of the Domestic Animals of Africa.* New York: Africana Publ. Corp.

ERMAN, ADOLF
1894   *Life in Ancient Egypt.* London: Macmillan.

FLANNERY, K.
1972   The Cultural Evolution of Civilizations. *Annual Review of Ecology and Systematics* 3:399-426.

FORBES, R. J.
1956   *Studies in Ancient Technology, Vol. IV.* Leiden: E. J. Brill.

FORD, J.
1962   A quantitative method for deriving cultural chronology. *Pan American Union Technical Manual 1.*

FRIEDMAN, J. and M. ROWLANDS, eds.
1978   *The Evolution of Social Systems.* Pittsburgh: University of Pittsburgh Press.

GADALLA, ABUL ELA
1924-   The Castor Oil Plant. *Agricultural Journal of Egypt* New Series, 1924-25. pp. 55-65.
1925

GAILLARD, C. and G. DARESSY
1905   *La Faune Momifiée de l'Antique Égypte.* Cairo.

GAUTHIER, H.
1925-   *Dictionnaire des noms géographiques contenus dans les textes hiéroglyphiques,* vol. I and
1931   vol. VI. Cairo.

GOLÉNISCHEFF, W.
1898   Pap. hiératique de la collection W. Golénischeff contenant la description du voyage de l'égyptien Ounou-Amon en Phénicie, *RdT* 21:74-102.

GOMAA, F.
1974   *Die libyshen Fürstentümer des Deltas von Tod Osorkons II. bis zur Wiedervereinigung ägyptens durch Psametik I.* Beihefte zum Tübinger Atlas des Vorderen Orients B/6, Weisbaden.

GRENFELL, B.
1901-   Graeco-Roman Egypt. In *Egypt Exploration Fund, Archaeological Reports:* 1903-03, pp. 1-3.
1903

GRENFELL, B., and A. HUNT
1906-   *The Hibeh Papyri,* Part I (nos. 1-171), Egypt Exploration Fund Graeco-Roman Branch VII,
1955   London 1906; Part II, by E. G. Turner, London 1955.

GRIFFITH, F. L.
1909   *Catalogue of the Demotic Papyri in the John Rylands Library Manchester.* 3 vols. Manchester.

HAMMOND, M.
1972   *The City in the Ancient World.* Cambridge: Harvard University Press.

HARRIS, M.
  1979   *Cultural Materialism: The Struggle for a Science of Culture*. New York: Random House.

HAYES, J.
  1972   *Late Roman Pottery: A Catalogue of Roman Fine Wares*. London.
  1975   *Roman and Pre-Roman Glass in the Royal Ontario Museum*. Toronto: Royal Ontario Museum.

HEDRICK, U. P. (ed.)
  1919   Sturtevant's Notes on Edible Plants. *Twenty-seventh Annual Report*, Vol. 2, Pt. II. Department of Agriculture, State of New York.

HELBAEK, HANS
  1958   Plant Economy. In *Ancient Lachish, Lachish IV: The Bronze Age*. The Wellcome Marston Archaeological Research Expedition to the Near East, Vol. IV. Ed. by Olga Tufnell. pp. 309-317.
  1969   Appendix I: Plant Collecting, Dry-Farming, and Irrigation Agriculture in Prehistoric Deh Luran. In *Prehistory and Human Ecology of the Deh Luran Plain. Memoirs of the Museum of Anthropology*. University of Michigan, No. 1. By Frank Hole, Kent V. Flannery and James A. Neely. pp. 383-424.
  1970   The Plant Husbandry of Hacilar. In *Excavations at Hacilar* by J. Mellaart. pp. 189-244. Edinburg: Edinburg University Press.

HELCK, W.
  1975   Wirtschaftsgeschichte Des Alten Ägypten. In *Handbuch Der Orientalistik*. Leiden: E. J. Brill.

HEMPEL, C.
  1959   The logic of functional analysis. In L. Gross, ed., *Symposium on Sociological Theory*. New York: Harper and Row.

HILZHEIMER, M.
  1941   *Animal Remains from Tell Asmar*. Oriental Institute, University of Chicago, Studies in Ancient Oriental Civilization, 20.

HODDER, I. and C. ORTON
  1976   *Spatial Analysis in Archaeology*. Cambridge: Cambridge University Press.

HOLSCHER, U.
  1954   *The excavations of Medinet Habu, v. post-Ramesside remains*. Chicago: University of Chicago, Oriental Institute Publications, LXVI.

HOWARD, M. M.
  1962   The Early Domestication of Cattle and the Determination of their Remains. *Zeit. Tierzüchtung und Züchtungsbiologie*, 76:252-265.

HUTCHINSON, R. W.
  1962   *Prehistoric Crete*. Harmondsworth: Penguin.

HUXLEY, J.
1956   Review of *Evolution, cultural and biological*, ed. W. Thomas. *Current Anthropology*.

IPPEL, A., and G. ROEDER
1921   Die Denkmäler des Pelizaeus-Museums zu Hildesheim (1921), 98-99, Abb. 35.

JOHNSON, G.
1977   Aspects of regional analysis in archaeology. *Annual Review of Anthropology* 6:479-508.

JONES, G.
1934   Control of Barley Diseases 1. Closed Smut. *Technical and Scientific Service, Mycological Service Bulletin*, No. 142. Ministry of Agriculture.

JOUKOWSKY, M.
1980   *Field Archaeology*. Englewood Cliffs: Prentice-Hall.

JUDGE, W., J. EBERT, and R. HITCHCOCK
1975   Sampling in Regional Archaeological Survey. In J. Mueller, ed., *Sampling in Archaeology*. Tucson: University of Arizona Press.

JUNKER, H.
1912   El Hibeh. *Anzeiger der Oesterreichische Akademie der Wissenschaften in Wien, Phil.-Hist. Klasse*, 49 (98-101).

KAMAL, A.
1901   Description générale des ruines de Hibé, de son temple et de sa necropole. *Annales du Service des Antiquités de l'Égypte* 2:84-91.

KEIMER, L.
1936   Bericht Uber in Maadi 1931 und 1933 Gefundene Samen. In *The Excavations of the Egyptian University in the Neolithic Site at Maadi, Second Preliminary Report, Season 1932*. Cairo: Egyptian University, Faculty of Arts.

KELLEY, A.
1976   *The Pottery of Ancient Egypt*. Toronto: Royal Ontario Museum.

KEMP, BARRY J.
1972   Temple and Town in Ancient Egypt. In *Man, Settlement, and Urbanism*. Ed. by Peter J. Ucko, Ruth Tringham, and G. W. Dimbleby. Cambridge, Massachusetts: Duckworth. pp. 657-680.
1977   The early development of towns in Egypt. *Antiquity* LI(203):185-200.

KENDALL, D.
1971   Seriation from abundance matrices. In F. R. Hodson, D. G. Kendall, and P. Tauty, eds., *Mathematics in the Archaeological and Historical Sciences*. Edinburgh: Edinburgh University Press.

KIENITZ, F.
1953   *Die politische Geschichte äegyptens vom 7. bis zum 4. Jahrhundert vor der Zeitwende*. Berlin.

KING, MARY ELIZABETH
1978   Analytical Methods and Prehistoric Textiles. *American Antiquity* 43:89-96.

KITCHEN, K.
1973   *The Third Intermediate Period in Egypt*. Warminster: Aris & Phillips.

KRAELING, C., and R. McC. ADAMS
1960   *City Invicible*. Chicago: University of Chicago Press.

LAKWETE, ANGELA
1977   Conservation Report: Meroitic, X-Group, and Christian Fabrics. ms.

LATTIMORE, O.
1951   *Inner Asian Frontiers of China*. Boston: Deacon.

LAUER, J. P., V. LAURENT-TÄCKHOLM, and E. ÅBERG
1950   Les Plantes Decouvertes dan les Souternains de L'Enceinte du Roi Zoser a Saggarah (IIIe
        Dynastie). *Du Bulletin de l'Institute d'Égypte* XXXII:127-157.

LUCAS, A.
1948   *Ancient Egyptian Materials & Industries*, 3rd. rev. ed. London: Edward Arnold.

LUCAS, A. and J. R. HARRIS
1962   *Ancient Egyptian Materials and Industries*. London: Edward Arnold.

MANSON-BAHR, P. H.
1966   *Manson's Tropical Diseases*. 16th ed. Baltimore: Williams and Wilkins.

MARQUARDT, W.
1978   Advances in archaeological seriation. In M. B. Schiffer, ed., *Advances in Archaeological Meth-
        od and Theory*, vol. 1, pp. 257-314. New York: Academic Press.

MAYER-THURMAN, CHRISTA C. and BRUCE WILLIAMS
1979   *Ancient Textiles from Nubia*. Chicago: The Art Institute.

MEYER, FREDERICK G.
1980   Carbonized Food Plants of Pompeii, Herculaneum, and the Villa at Torre Annunziata. *Eco-
        nomic Botany* 34(4):401-437.

MONTET, PIERRE
1981   *Everyday Life in Egypt*. Philadelphia: University of Pennsylvania Press.

MUELLER, J., ed.
1975   *Sampling in Archaeology*. Tucson: University of Arizona Press.

O'CONNOR, D.
1972   A Regional Population in Egypt to circa 600 B.C. In *Population Growth: Anthropological
        Implications*. Cambridge (Mass.): MIT Press.
1974   Political systems and archaeological data in Egypt: 2600-1780 B.C. *World Archaeology* 6:
        15-38.

OSBORN, DALE J.
1968   Notes on Medicinal and Other Uses of Plants in Egypt. *Economic Botany* 22:165-177.

OSBORN, D. J. and I. HELMY
1980   The Contemporary Land Mammals of Egypt (Including Sinai). *Fieldiana, Zool.*, New Series, 5.

PARIBENI, E.
1935   Rapporto preliminare su gli scavi di Hibeh. *Aegyptus* 15:385-404.

PARSONS, J.
1971   *Prehistoric Settlement Patterns in the Texcoco Region, Mexico.* Memoirs of the Museum of Anthropology, University of Michigan, No. 3.

PETRIE, W.
1904   *Roman Ehnasya (Herakleopolis Magna).* London: Special Extra Publication of the Egypt Exploration Fund.

PIA, J.
1942   Untersuchtungen über die Rassenzugehörigkeit der altägyptischen Hausschafes. *Zeit. Tierzüchtung und Züchtungsbiologie.* Vol. 51.

PLOG, S.
1976   Relative efficiencies of sampling techniques for archaeological surveys. In K. Flannery, ed., *The Early Mesoamerican Village*, pp. 136-158. New York: Academic Press.
1978   Sampling in archaeological surveys. *American Antiquity* 43(2):280-285.

PORTER, B., and R. MOSS
        Topographical Bibliography of Ancient Egyptian Hieroglyphic Texts, Reliefs, and Paintings, Vol. IV, p. 124-125. Oxford: Griffith Institute.

RAGAB, HASSAN
1980   Contribution à l'étude du Papyrus (*Cyperus papyrus* L.) et à sa Transformation en support de l'écriture (papyrus des anciens). Thèse pour le grade de Docteur de L'I.N.P.G. A L'Institut National Polytechnique de Grenoble.

RANKE, H.
1926   *Koptische Friedhofe bei Karara und der Amontempel Scheschonks I. bei el Hibe.* Berlin.

REDDING, RICHARD
n.d.   "The Faunal Remains." In R. Wenke and M. E. Lane, eds., *Land of the Lake: Preliminary Report of the Fayyum Archaeological Project.*

REED, CLYDE F.
1977   *Economically Important Foreign Weeds in the United States.* U.S.D.A. *Agricultural Handbook*, No. 498. Washington, D.C.

RENFREW, JANE M.
1973   *Paleoethnobotany: The Prehistoric Food Plants of the Near East and Europe.* New York: Columbia University Press.

ROSTOVTSEV, M.
    1941   *The Social and Economic History of the Hellenistic World.* Oxford: Oxford University Press.

RUFFER, SIR ARMAND
    1919   Foods in Egypt. *Mémoires à L'Institut d'Égypte*, Vol. 1.

SAID, R.
    1981   *The Geological Evolution of the River Nile.* New York: Springer.

SCHIFFER, M.
    1976   *Behavioral Archaeology.* New York: Academic Press.

SERVICE, E.
    1975   *The Origins of Civilization and the State.* New York: Norton.

SHARER, R. and W. ASHMORE
    1979   *Fundamentals of Archaeology.* Menlo Park (Calif.): Benjamin/Cummings.

SHEIKHOLESLAMI, C. (with R. WENKE)
    1978   El-Hibeh Project, Research Development Trip. A Grant Proposal submitted to the Smithsonian
            Foreign Currency Program.

SJOBERG, G.
    1960   *The Preindustrial City.* New York: The Free Press.

SMITH, H.
    1976   "Aspects of the study of the Egyptian city," Abstract of a paper presented at the First Inter-
            national Congress of Egyptology, Cairo, Oct. 2-10.

SMITH, P. and T. CUYLER YOUNG, JR.
    1972   The Evolution of early agriculture and culture in greater Mesopotamia: A trial model. In Brian
            Spooner, ed., *Population Growth: Anthropological Implications.* Cambridge (Mass.): MIT
            Press.

SPALINGER, A.
    1976   Psammetichus, King of Egypt: I. *Journal of the American Research Center in Egypt* 13:133-
            147.

SPIEGELBERG, W.
            Briefe der 21. Dynastie aus El Hibe. *Zeitschrift für Agyptische Sprache* 53:1-30, 16 Abbil-
            dunger, Tafel I-VII.

SPOONER, B., ed.
    1972   *Population Growth: An Anthropological Perspective.* Cambridge (Mass.): MIT Press.

STAFFE, A.
    1938   Über einen Hausschweinschädel aus dem früh-dynastischen Ägypten. *Zeit. Tierzüchtung und
            Züchtunsbiologie.* Vol. 41.

STEWARD, J.
  1949   Cultural causality and law: A trial formulation of the development of early civilizations. *American Anthropologist* 51:1-27.

TÄCKHOLM, VIVI
  1961   Botanical Identification of the Plants Found at the Monastery of Phoebammon. In *Le Monastère de Phoebammon dans le Thébaide* Tombe III. Publications de la Societe D'Archeologie Copte. Rapports de Fouille. pp. 1-38.
  1974   *Students' Flora of Egypt*, Second Edition. Cairo: Cairo University Press.

TÄCKHOLM, V. and MOHAMMAD DRAR
  1950   Flora of Egypt, Vol. 2. *Bulletin of the Faculty of Science*, No. 28, Fouad I University, Cairo.

TÄCKHOLM, V., GUNNAR TÄCKHOLM, and MOHAMMAD DRAR
  1941   Flora of Egypt, Vol. I. *Bulletin of the Faculty of Science*, No. 17, Fouad I University, Cairo.

TOUSSOUN, O.
  1923   Anciennes branches du Nil. *Memoire de l'Institute de l'Égypte.*
  1925   Memorie sur l'histoire du Nil. *Memoire de l'Institute de l'Égypte* 8-10; 1-543.

TRIGGER, B.
  1979   Egypt and the comparative study of early civilizations. In K. Weeks, ed., *Egyptology and the Social Sciences.* Cairo: The American University in Cairo Press.

UCKO, P., R. TRINGHAM, and G. DIMBLEBY, eds.
  1972   *Man, Settlement and Urbanism.* London: Duckworth.

VAN ZEIST, WILLEM
  1976   On Macroscopic Traces of Food Plants in Southwestern Asia. *Philosophical Transactions of the Royal Society, London Bulletin* 275:25-41.

VON DEN DRIESCH, A.
  1976   *A Guide to the Measurement of Animal Bones from Archaeological Sites. Peabody Mus., Bull.*, 1.

WAINWRIGHT, G.
  1927   El Hibah and esh Shurafa and their connection with Herakleopolis and Cusae. *Annales du Service des Antiquitiés de l'Égypte.* XXVII:76-104.
  1944   Studies in the Petition of Peteese. *Bulletin of the John Rylands Library* 28, no. 1:228-271.

WALLACE, DWIGHT
  1975   The Analysis of Weaving Patterns: Examples from the Early Periods in Peru. In P. Fiske, ed., *Irene Emery Roundtable on Museum Textiles, 1974 Proceedings*, pp. 101-116. Washington, D.C.: The Textile Museum.

WENDORF, F. and R. SCHILD
  1976   *Prehistory of the Nile Valley.* New York: Academic Press.

WENKE, R.

1975-   Imperial investments and agricultural developments in Parthian and Sasanian Khuzestan:
1976   150 B.C. to A.D. *Mesopotamia* XXI:31-221.

1980   Explaining the Evolution of Cultural Complexity: A Review. In M. Schiffer, ed., *Advances in Archaeological Method and Theory* vol. 4, pp. 79-119. New York: Academic Press.

1981   The El-Hibeh Project: Preliminary Report of the 1980 Season. Seattle, University of Washington, ms.

WENKE, R. and M. E. LANE

n.d.   *Land of the Lake: Preliminary Report of the Fayyum Archaeological Project.* In Preparation.

WETTERSTROM, WILMA

1982   Plant Remains. In *Quseir Al-Qadim 1980. Preliminary Report.* Malibu: Undena Publications. pp. 355-377.

In   Paleoethnobotanical Studies at Predynastic Sties in the Nagada-Khattara Region. In F. A.
Press.   Hassan, ed., *Predynastic Studies in the Nagada-Khattara Region of Upper Egypt.* New York: Academic Press.

WHEATLEY, P.

1971   *The Pivot of the Four Quarters.* Chicago: Aldine.

WHITCOMB, D. and J. JOHNSON

1979   *Quseir Al-Qadim 1978: Preliminary Report.* Cairo: American Research Center in Egypt, Inc.

1982   *Quseir Al-Qadim 1980: Preliminary Report.* Malibu: Undena Publications.

WIEBE, G. A.

1979   Barley: Origin, Botany, Culture, Winter Hardiness, Genetics, Utilization, Pests. In *Barley: Origin, Botany, Culture, Winter Hardiness, Genetics, Utilization, Pests. Agriculture Handbook*, Number 338. U.S. Department of Agriculture. pp. 1-9.

WILD, J. P.

1970   *Textile Manufacture in the Northern Roman Provinces*, Cambridge: Cambridge University Press.

WILSON, J.

1951   *The Culture of Ancient Egypt.* Chicago: University of Chicago Press.

1960   Civilization without cities. In C. Kraeling and R. McC. Adams, eds., *City Invincible.* Chicago: The University of Chicago Press.

WISHART, E.

1975   *Clustan IC user manual.* London: Computer Centre, University College, London.

WITTFOGEL, K.

1957   *Oriental Despotism: A comparative study of total power.* New Haven: Yale University Press.

WRIGHT, H. T.

1977   Recent research on the origin of the state. *Annual Review of Anthropology* 6:379-397.

WRIGHT, H. T. and G. JOHNSON
  1975   Population, exchange, and early state formation in southwestern Iran. *American Anthropologist* 77:267-289.

YOFFEE, N.
  1979   The decline and rise of Mesopotamian Civilization: An ethnoarchaeological perspective on the evolution of social complexity. *American Antiquity* 44(1):5-35.

YOUNG, T.
  1972   Population densities and early Mesopotamian origins. In P. Ucko, et al., eds., *Man, Settlement and Urbanism*. London: Duckworth.

ZEUNER, F. E.
  1963   *A History of the Domesticated Animals*. Hutchinson: London.

ZOHARY, DANIEL and MARIA HOPF
  1973   Domestication of Pulses in the Old World. *Science* 182(4115):887-894.

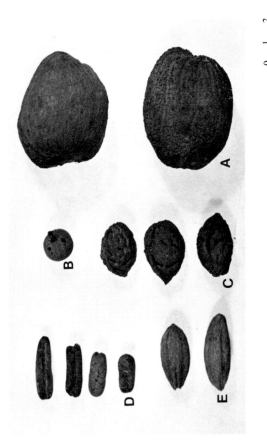

PLATE 5.3

FRUITS. A. Dom (*Hyphaene thebaica*) fruit. B. Sycamore Fig (*Ficus sycomorus*) fruit. C. Peach (*Prunus persica*) stone. D. Date (*Phoenix dactylifera*) stone.

PLATE 5.4

FRUITS. A. Egyptian plum (*Cordia myxa*) stones. B. Persea (*Minusops schimperi*) seeds. C. Watermelon (*Citrullus lunatus*) seeds. D. Carob (*Certonia siliqua*) seeds. E. Christ's thorn (*Ziziphus spina-christi*) stone.

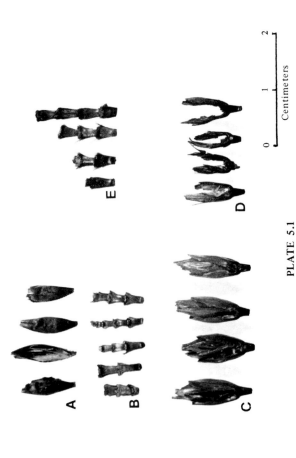

PLATE 5.1

CEREALS. A. Barley (*Hordeum vulgare*) grain. B. Barley rachis segment C. Emmer Wheat (*Triticum dicoccocum*) spikelet. D. Emmer wheat internode. E. Hard Wheat (*Triticum durum*) rachis segment.

PLATE 5.2

OIL PLANTS. A. Olive (*Olea europaea*) stone. B. Flax (*Linum usitatissimum*) capsule. C. Castor Bean (*Ricinus communis*). D. Sesame (*Sesamum indicum* or *S. orientale*) capsule.

I

PLATE 5.5

SEASONINGS AND NUTS. A. Coriander (*Coriandrum sativum*) capsule. B. Pine cone (*Pinus pinea*) scale.

PLATE 5.6

WILD PLANTS. A. Sedge (*Cyperus* sp.) rhyzome. B. Acacia (*Acacia nilotic*) seeds and pod.

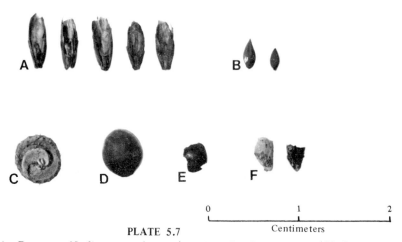

PLATE 5.7

WEEDS. A. Ryegrass (*Lolium temulentum*) grain. B. Canary grass (*Phalaris paradoxa*) grain. C. Medick (*Medicago hispida*) pod. D. Yellow vetchling (*Lathyrus aphaca*) seed. E. Vetch (*Vicia lutea*) seed. F. cf. Gromwell (*Buglossoides*) nutlet.

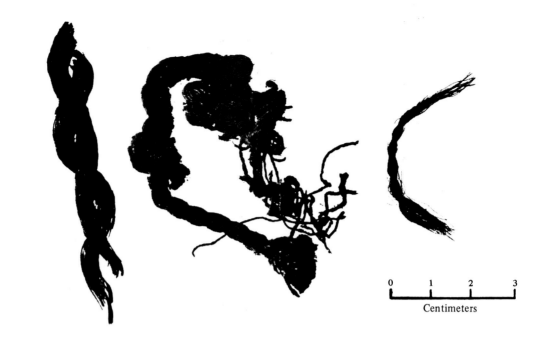

PLATE 6.1
Examples of cordage showing a range of diameters.
Left to right: Unidentified hard fiber (B97 P1); linen (B106 P1); unidentified hairlike fiber (B53 P25).

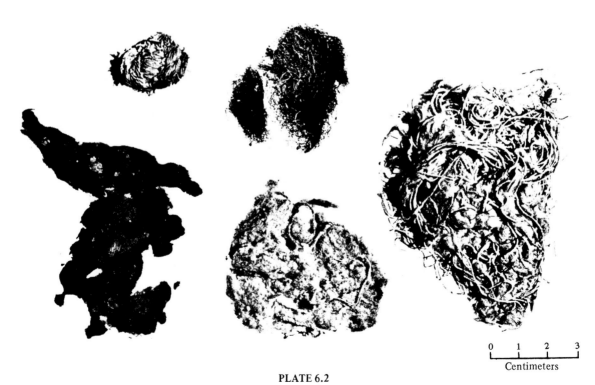

PLATE 6.2
Examples of different types of massed fibers.
Upper row, left to right: ball of yarn (B43 P1); hairy fibers (B8 P1). Bottom row, left to right:
green felt (B54 P2); mass of fibrous material (B31 P1); fibrous material associated with cordage (B17 P35).

IV

PLATE 6.4

Variety in faced plain weaves in terms of thread counts and yarn diameters. Left: warp faced striped fragment, blue and beige (B50 P3). Right, top: yellow fragment (B35 P3); bottom: weft faced fragment with selvage (B77 P30).

PLATE 6.3

Variety in balanced plain woven structures in terms of thread counts and yarn diameters. Upper row, left to right: beige fragment, seamed edge (B37 P9); blue cotton fragment. Lower row, left to right: yellow linen fragment (B44 P1); fragment with corded selvage (B44 P4); yellow fragment with purple stripe (B44 P9).

PLATE 6.5
Tapestry woven fragment in beige and blue (B82 P4).

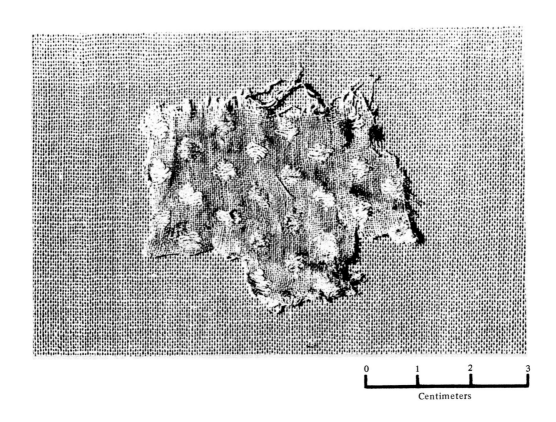

PLATE 6.6
Plain woven beige cotton fabric with lozenges in supplementary weft (B70 P3).

VI

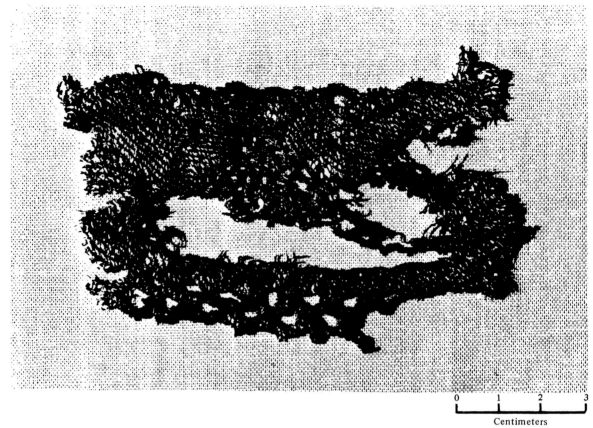

PLATE 6.7
Yellow wool fragment; possibly twined or plaited (B53 P30).

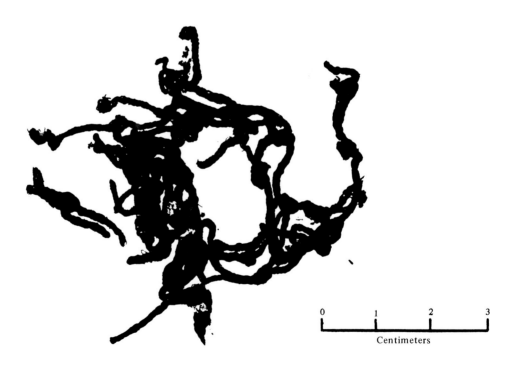

PLATE 6.8
Knotted cordage (B31 P1).

PLATE 6.10
Beige fragment with plied warp ends forming fringe.
Loops remain in some warp ends (B35 P26).

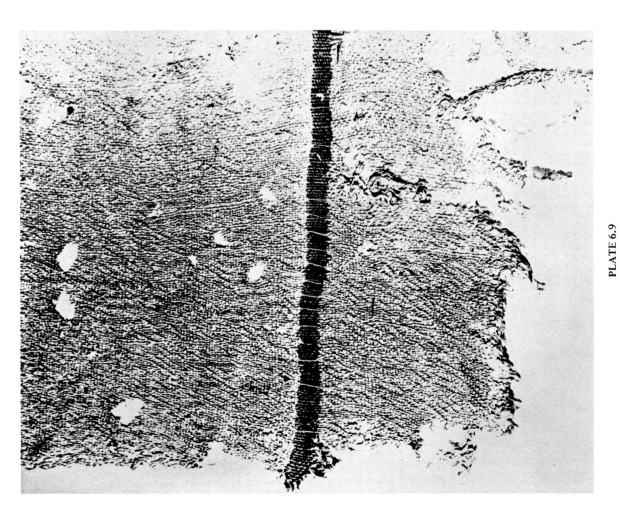

PLATE 6.9
Large yellow wool fragment with purple stripe in weft.
Stitching and selvage present. Note warp floats over stripe.
Surface texture results from differences in degree of twist of the yarns (B33 P1).

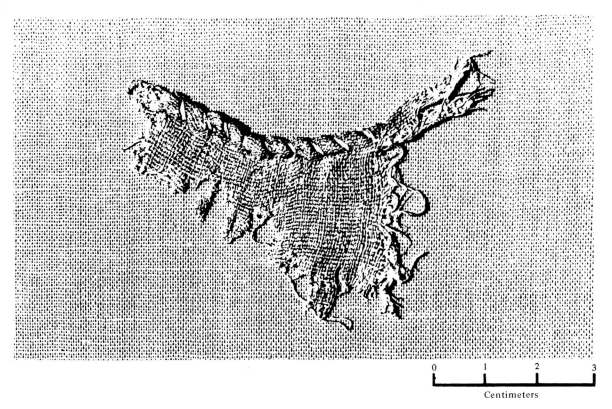

PLATE 6.11
Beige fragment exhibiting shaped edge and hemstitching (B84 P14).

PLATE 6.12
Folded and seamed fragment, yellow with purple stripes (B52 P1).

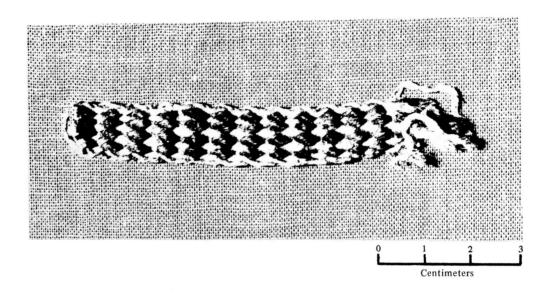

PLATE 6.13
Narrow linen band with both side selvages present. Beige and brown (B97 P2).

PLATE 6.14
Remains of a small lizard enclosed in a textile.

PLATE Appendix 3.1
Papyri fragments from TS1

A

B

PLATE Appendix 3.2
Stamped Bricks: (A) ["high priest of] Amun
[Men]kheper [re]" c. 18 cm x 15 xm, from TS1a,
Wall B, Building I; (B) "Pinudjem and Estemkheb,"
c. 38 cm x 20 cm, from near Enclosure Wall.

PLATE Appendix 3.3

Miscellaneous inscribed objects.

(A) pot sherd inscribed in Greek or Coptic, about 8.5 cm x 7.0 cm, from TS1d;

(B) base of lamp with inscription, c. 12 cm x 7 cm, from TS1d.

PLATE Appendix 4.1

Small finds: (A) fragment of faience ring; (B) fragment of faience pendant bead in flower shape;

(C) fragment of faience amulet; (D) drilled agate bead; (E) fragment of faience Udgat "eye";

(F) fragment of faience object. All of these objects are from Test Square 1 in disturbed contexts.

XII

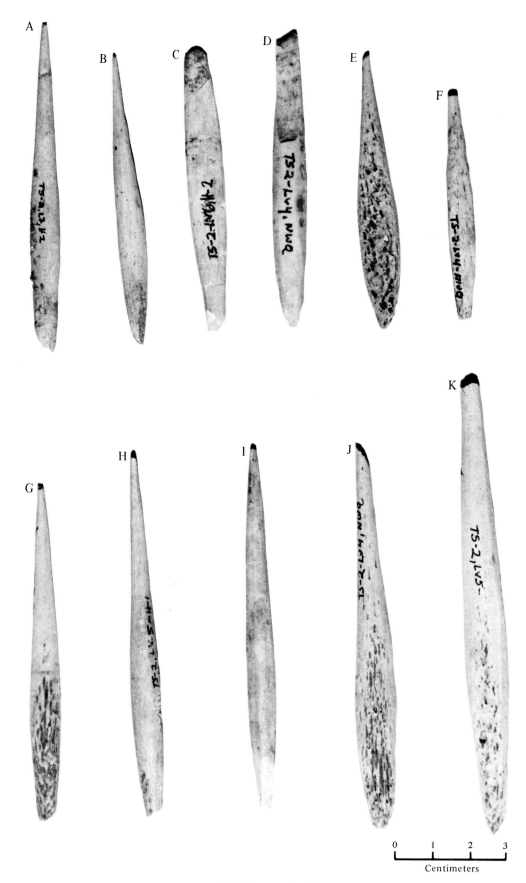

PLATE Appendix 4.2
Worked bone objects. All from fill in Test Square 2.